# THE ENTREPRENEURS BUSINESS CLUB

A Guide for Entrepreneurs by Entrepreneurs

By Entrepreneurs for Entrepreneurs!

# **E**ntrepreneurs **B**usiness **C**lub

For Entrepreneurs

by

Entrepreneurs

Copyright © 2017 Ash Lawrence

All rights reserved.

ISBN: 1976318343
ISBN-13: 978-1976318344

# DEDICATION

This book is dedicated to all of those hard working small business owners who are being too busy to earn any money, just to show you that there is another way!

# CONTENTS

|    | Acknowledgements | i   |
|----|------------------|-----|
| 1  | Introduction     | 1   |
| 2  | **S**trategy     | 5   |
| 3  | **Y**ou          | 24  |
| 4  | **S**tand Out    | 36  |
| 5  | **T**en out of 10| 58  |
| 6  | **E**ngage       | 69  |
| 7  | **M**ethod       | 89  |
| 8  | **S**ervice      | 107 |
| 9  | The People       | 125 |
| 10 | Resources        | 149 |

# ACKNOWLEDGEMENTS

Carrie Stay
Chris Verbiest
Deborah Jones
Emily Hackett
Rachel Cowell
Roland Stanley
Ross Cowan
Sally Marshall

# *1 INTRODUCTION*

This book is a series of personal lessons from a group of successful business owners, (The **E**ntrepreneurs **B**usiness **C**lub), and myself, who would like to share with you, our experience of owning our own businesses. As you work your way through the book you will find lots of valuable lessons that, if actioned, will make a major difference to you, your business and your life!

There is however, one very big proviso! YOU MUST **TAKE ACTION** on what you learn. Visualisation, positive thinking and the law of attraction are all very good and highly recommended but ONLY if you also take massive action on what you learn.

Action really is the cure to most things in life. Sitting still and waiting for things to happen is a recipe for disaster. As you work your way through the book you will find some really useful tips and if you are worried about how to action them, contact the person that authored that particular subject, (their details are at the back of the book). They will welcome talking to you, because they know how important having a mentor is to the ongoing success for any person or business.

I suppose you could say that my first mentor was my dad, who taught me that I had to work if I wanted money. There was no such thing as pocket money, only effort and reward or as I now like to refer to it as cause and effect.

My dad used to grow tomato plants from seed in a glass homemade miniature green house on the balcony of our flat. I then used to go around the council estate in East London with all of these young tomato plants on my go-cart which my dad had made from a disused scaffold board and wheels from an old pram that someone had left standing by the rubbish chute. I charged people sixpence per plant and then my dad would give me half of the takings. This was my first experience of cause and effect; you sell or do something, you get money or goods in exchange!

My dad taught un-armed combat in the police force, which, for me was brilliant as I learned to look after myself very early on in life. Martial arts, as far as my dad was concerned, was all about self-discipline and being controlled with your personal actions and emotions at all times. (I'll tell you more about how this applies to business later in the book).

Attending seven different infant and primary schools in six years did absolutely nothing for my education. However, it was wonderful for my life skills, which, I now realise have played a major part in the success I have enjoyed in business.

My next mentor was my best mate Jamie's dad, Ben. I was an apprentice plumbing & heating engineer working for his business. He was the only person that would employ me because I didn't have any formal qualifications, so it was good for me that he believed, *"Hire for attitude, train for skills!"* This is something that I full heartedly agree with today, as a positive attitude will take you a lot further than a great education with a poor attitude.

Ben's first lesson for me was about building long term relationships. He taught me early on the old adage that we have all heard, *"It's not what you know but who you know!"* In the beginning I wasn't sure what that meant but I went out of my way to find out! I now know that it is not only about the people that you know, and how well you know them but more importantly, how well they know you.

Understanding numbers was another big lesson from Ben. He used to say to me, *"If you don't look after the numbers they won't look after you!"* When I look back over the years and see the amount of people that I've met that had their own business and it failed because they had absolutely no concept of the numbers it amazes me! Like a lot of things people make excuses about the things that they don't like doing and that is why a great mentor is essential for all of us, to ensure that we understand and action the things that need to be done. You will learn in this book why the numbers are important and how to ensure that you are looking at them in the right way in your business.

My next mentor was a Dale Carnegie trainer and he helped me understand myself and brought home the only thing that I learned at school and that was something I'm sure you've heard of too… *"Every action has an equal and opposite reaction!"* Basically cause and effect! You can't plant bananas and pick cucumbers. He would consistently tell me that I had to change me before I could change anything else and he gave me the tools to do that. If you believe that making money, being happy or getting what you want is hard; guess what? It will be!

In order for us to change anything we have to be aware that we need to change, and that is one of the problems - most small business owners are not fully aware of what needs to change to get a better result in their business.

Generally things just don't change on their own, you have to take action. *"It's not until the pain of the same is greater than the pain of change will we actually change!"* If you are not aware of a weakness you can't turn it into a strength.

By Entrepreneurs for Entrepreneurs!

This book will give you an insight into the seven key areas in any business and then you can assess your own business against these seven areas:

**S**trategy
**Y**ou
**S**tand out
**T**en out of 10
**E**ngage
**M**ethod
**S**ervice

As you work your way through each chapter score yourself on a scale of one to ten, where one is, no you haven't got any of those things in your business and ten you've got it all. Be honest otherwise you won't get a result.

If you score;
1-3 it's a cross
4-7 it's a neutral
8-10 is a tick

By doing this it will give you a clue as to where you really need to focus your efforts in your business.

I can't recommend enough that you find yourself a coach, mentor or accountability group to help you grow in business and in life.

Now go on and enjoy this book and above all else take ACTION on the things that you learn!

### *Ash Lawrence*

## 2 STRATEGY

*There are so many great quotes for strategy… "Fail to plan, plan to fail!" "If you don't know where you are going how will you know when you get there!" "If you're not working towards your goals the chances are you will be working towards someone else's!" The list goes on and on and the chances are you don't have a plan either…* **Ash**

I have spent the last 8 years empowering people with the tools they need so they can do amazing things. As a personal trainer you get to meet a wide range of people of all ages, professions and abilities. What this does is give you a brilliant insight to people's lives. They come to you to get fitter, lighter, stronger etc, and most importantly you build relationships with these people and you become great friends.

There is a moment when you see a client's eyes change, every belief about what they thought possible around food, training and achievement has just vanished in an instant. You have just empowered them, now they believe anything is possible and their life will never be the same again. This is the moment that gets you out of bed at 6am on a cold morning, the reason WHY you chose this career in the first place.

Standing on the finish line at a tough mudder, (12 mile obstacle course where they dunk you in ice water and electrocute you), with your client that's broken into tears of joy, who, just 12 months ago was about to lose their job in the police force because they couldn't run 200m, is one of the proudest moments in my career.

I have been blessed to help 100's of people achieve everything from crossing the finish line at the London Marathon to simply getting into that pair of jeans that they've paid too much money for, haven't been able to get into for years and getting the top button done up! What I love is that every challenge, every journey is as completely unique and individual as the client you're working with.

There's no one size fits all solution and no magic pill to make you healthily drop 10lb's in a week (although there are many that can make you do that but I strongly wouldn't advise them).

Here's the thing, no matter how different the person, circumstance or result is, for it to be successful they must all follow the same process. Before we ever touch a weight, discuss food or even lace up a trainer, we always sit down and set goals. This is by far the most important part of the whole process. No-one ever just 'finds themselves' on the finish line at a tough mudder or 10lb's lighter by accident.

It takes planning, determination, knowledge and an understanding that it will never go exactly to plan, but that's OK. Working out how to overcome all of these inevitable challenges is what makes it fun and what allows you as a professional to stand out from the crowd in your industry.

Having this mindset will rapidly grow your business. Mine went from a weekend boot camp in a field to a private studio with 7 coaches on board and online coaching company that hosts events, sells e-books and helps change the lives of people from all over the country.

All this happened in less than 4 years and the biggest thing that l learned is, that no matter how much you set goals for other people, if you don't set them for yourself and your business, you are destined to fail!

Here's a little stat that you may find interesting;

- 80% of people in the UK do not set goals
- 15% set goals but don't write them down
- 3% write them but don't review them
- Only 2% write them down and review their goals

Is it any wonder that only 2% of the population earn more than £100,000 a year?

If you are a reading this you are a business owner or at the very least seriously thinking about it. If you are thinking about it, then **DO IT NOW!** There is nothing more rewarding than setting up on your own. That being said, if you ask any business owner if it's easy, then the answer will almost always be no, but so worth it. The graph from start up to success is not a straight line. It has massive peaks and troughs. The only way you can be successful is to accept that you are going fail, a lot, but you must understand that all of your best growth and learnings come from making these mistakes.

"It's only a mistake if you do it twice, otherwise it's a beautiful lesson."

The key to this is learning from these mistakes and moving forward. My mentor and good friend Ash Lawrence describes the process of people repeating the same unsuccessful behaviours as "a form of mental illness."

My first business failed massively after a very successful first 2 years. This was caused by the complete breakdown of the relationship between my old business partner and I. Working in a business surrounded by 7 staff and 100's of happy clients, while you argue with your business partner, feels like one of the loneliest places in the world.

## By Entrepreneurs for Entrepreneurs!

This is well behind me now and my new business now has the potential to positively affect millions of people. While I was 'in' the day to day grind of my old business it was impossible to get out of the detail and step 'out' to see the big picture of while it was failing. When I look back now its very simple and clear to see …. we hadn't set our goals properly!

As with most startups you'll go through the first year running on 90% excitement and 10% strategy. You're taking on all challenges, reacting as you go, full of enthusiasm and you know what …. it works! The problem is with so much going on and things constantly changing you spend very little time keeping track of, well, everything. You spend money hand over fist, never really put a structure into your business and when you start to really build momentum, you become overwhelmed and then your clients start to suffer. These are of course details that can be easily overcome but when you add in the 'mismatch of expectations' from the owners about what happens when these things occur, who is responsible for what or even "whose fault is that?", things deteriorate quickly.

Ultimately we failed because we didn't clearly set goals and expectations at the beginning. People change, businesses evolve and money has a massive impact. If you are not super clear at the beginning then you can be damn sure that when all the other stuff happens there will be nothing but a shit storm coming your way!

This was my beautiful lesson and something that I won't be repeating again.

The best thing is, this is really easy to avoid, and one of the most fun parts of starting a business. Goal setting will improve your life, your relationships and your business.

Here's my top strategies for setting life changing goals ....

## Set an emotionally charged goal!

In my industry the most common request from a client is, "I want to lose weight". My first response to this is always, "you're gonna have to do better than that". Losing weight as a goal is frankly limp. It has no back bone, no substance, nothing specific and you can guarantee that it won't work!

I always go in hard with my clients at this point because I know that the next half hour is make or break whether they are successful or not. By asking people why they want to lose weight, (you need to appreciate they won't tell you the real reason straight away), if you dig a little deeper and really get to heart of it you will get an answer. Like one client who eventually said "because I'm the oldest dad at my daughters primary school and I want to kick all the other dad's arses in the dad's race on her school sports day". This is perfect because you now have something specific, time bound and most importantly something emotionally charged! What do you think the chances are of him hitting his goal and making his daughter proud against simply, 'losing weight'?

You need to be seriously emotionally charged about your business! If you are not, you will be outperformed and left for dust by one of your competitors that are truly passionate about what they do. I truly believe that if you are not in business to change lives then you shouldn't be in business.

I understand that some businesses may not be as sexy as personal training your client to cross the finish line at a tough mudder, but even if your business is fixing photocopiers and you are striving to deliver the best quality service you can guarantee that will be life changing to your client. No matter what you're having a positive impact!

Get to the heart of why you do what you do, who you want to help and how you are going to feel when you do it. There is an awesome book by Simon Sinek called 'Start with Why' I seriously recommend that you read it.

## Start with the end in mind!

"If you're not being proactive you're being reactive."

When driving to a new place, the first thing you do is set the destination on your sat nav. You wouldn't get in and just start driving because you don't know which direction you need to go. This is why you need to be super clear on what the outcome of your business is, otherwise you are just driving around aimlessly. Just like a sat nav that goes off route, you can constantly re-adjust to keep yourself on track, but without the destination all you will end up doing is reacting to situations as and when they happen. This will keep you busy but is pointless if you're wanting to grow.

Once you've created an emotionally charged goal for your business you need to put a timescale on it. I do this with my clients because it's an excellent motivator plus it allows you to reverse engineer the process of how you are going to do it. A client getting married in 6 months who wants to lose 3 dress sizes can break down that goal into smaller bitesize chunks (1 dress size every 2 months). You can now do the same thing with your business but obviously your world domination will take slightly longer than 6 months so we'll start at 10 years.

Set the goal for 10 years then write down where you would need to be at year 5,3,2,1 and finally where you want to be in 6 months. Put this up on a wall where you can see it every day. Now you have a guide to keep you on track, remember only 3% of people actually review their goals so make sure you check in on your progress.

Two things I can promise you is that when you're focused, the goals you set as 5 year goals will be smashed in 3 and what you set out at the beginning will change and evolve over time but keep reviewing this process and I guarantee it will end up a much better version.

## Create a visual representation of your future!

Putting your 10 year plan on the wall will inspire you when times are tough but having a vision board that you see every morning when you wake up will turbo charge your efforts!

Did you know that every thought process you have starts as an image in your mind? If a picture can speak 1000 words then a carefully selected image can evoke powerful emotions, and instantly change your state by firing up your senses. These types of images are very powerful tools when it comes to motivation and exactly what you need to be seeing every day.

Get yourself something you can put on your wall and attach pictures to. Find images that represent your emotionally charged goal; what car you want, what house you want to live in, what companies you want to work with, people you want to help and anything that excites you! If it doesn't excite you, it doesn't go on; remember this is about creating an emotional attachment and anchoring these images in your head.

Lastly put it in your room, in your office or wherever it needs to be so that you see it every day. Trust me, it will change your life.

## Hold yourself accountable!

*"People don't pay for information, they pay for implementation!"*

It is a common misconception that information is power. I know personal trainers that purposely hold back giving away fitness tips when having normal conversations, because they feel they should be paid for it. This is of course a nonsense! Any person, anytime, anywhere can find out anything they need to know on their phone.

If this is the case then why isn't everyone ripped with a perfect beach body? It's because all the information in the world is nothing without someone holding you accountable and keeping you on track. Accountability is everything.

The reason I'm writing this book is because of a mentor and a group of entrepreneurs that all keep me motivated and kick my arse when I don't do what I say I'm going to do! Luckily there are loads of accountability groups and mentors out there that can help keep you on track.

That being said, be careful to make sure you're getting good advice and support otherwise it will be like the blind leading the blind and that's not good for anyone. A good mentor will come highly recommended from multiple sources, have a great track record and plenty of experience. If they're not ticking these boxes keep looking.

When you find a great mentor and group you will become part of something bigger than any one business. That's when you can truly start to make an impact, build relationships and contribute beyond yourself.

### *Ross Cowan*

Strategy is basically your road map for your business. It's the journey from where you are now to where you want to be. If you think about any other journey, you'd plan where you want to go before you set off. Your business is no different. That might sound quite daunting right now, if you are very ambitious and have big dreams of where you want your business to go, but the key is to take it one step at a time.

Nothing happens instantly or overnight despite what you read in the papers. Great things happen from a great deal of work behind the scenes over a longer period of time. This could be many years with a few false starts. In fact the most successful business people have often had several businesses with a few which didn't quite work. The key is to learn from those failures and use the lessons to build the next business.

So how do you get started?

Sit down and work out what you really want from your business. You might want to do this with your partner or family as well, so that they understand what you are working towards and are there to support you. A great way to get started is by creating a vision board. This is a fun activity you can do with all the family because it relates to your personal life as well as your business. You can't really split the two and your business determines your lifestyle. When you have a fabulous business you can have a fabulous lifestyle!

People often say that they aren't focused on money but we all need money to pay the bills and put food on the table. You might want to think of your goals in terms of a sum of money you need every month, or you might want to think about the things you can do with the money e.g. house, car, holidays etc. Either way, just do what works for you. The main thing is that you know why you are getting up in the morning and what it is you are working towards.

So let's take this one step at a time. Once you have a goal, then you need to break it down into small chunks which are easy to manage and not so daunting that you give up on day one!

As an example, we will take a financial goal of say £1,000 income each and every month. What do you need to do in your business to achieve that? The first thing to look at is your customers.

- How many customers do you need in order to achieve that figure?
- What is the average sale per customer?
- What is the average profit per customer?
- How many customers do you have now each month?
- Where do you find your customers?
- What do you need to do to increase your customers?

That probably sounds like quite a lot of work but take each one and have a good look at the numbers. A spreadsheet would be a good way to monitor this and then you can follow your progress and put the numbers into a chart so that you can see how close you are getting to your target.

In order to work all this out, you will need to have a good database and accounting system which gives you the information you need. If you don't have this in place already, then your first job is to get your paperwork in order! Going forward, knowing your numbers is going to be key and the easier you can make this process, the better it will be.

By Entrepreneurs for Entrepreneurs!

Your accounting system will give you a lot of this information, particularly if you're using a cloud-based accounts package. All your customers will be in there and you should be able to run reports showing customers, how often they buy from you, what they buy etc. and from this you can get the numbers to start building your strategy.

Once you have the information about your customers, you can look at where your best customers come from. It may be that your networking activities bring in all your leads. For some it will be referrals from happy customers and for others it could be from social media activity.

If we look at each of these in turn;

**Networking** – this can be a slow burn but regular and consistent networking will start to fill up your pipeline as long as you engage with people rather than sell at them. People buy from those they know, like and trust so when they are ready to buy, they will come back to you. Obviously they don't all want your product or service on the day you meet them, so it can be a slow process. However, once you start to get customers, they will tell others. Encourage them to give you testimonials and make sure you give them testimonials for anything you have purchased from them.

**Referrals** – this is a great way to build your business and it is much cheaper to retain regular customers and get referrals than keep looking for new customers. If you aren't doing it already, then ask your regular customers to refer you to their business contacts and friends. Depending on your business, this is a great way to keep your pipeline going. Some businesses offer an incentive for referrals and this is something you could consider.

When people are looking to buy a service or product, they tend to look at your website or review sites to see what other people say about you. Make sure that you have testimonials on your website and if you get a review which isn't so great, respond to it immediately so that you put right whatever the problem is. If you do this, then it will appear much better to anyone looking to potentially buy from you.

**Social media** – this is an interesting one. Social media is an extension of your face to face networking. Having an online presence is not enough. You still need to engage with people and chat to them. Personally I sell quite a few books just from talking to people online and asking what their challenges are. You need consistency with social media as well. Build your network before you need it and engage with people on social media. Work out where your customers are so if you are looking to sell to businesses you need to be on LinkedIn. You can also post blogs on LinkedIn which generate lots of views and connections.

Your strategy should therefore include a regular blog post together with connecting to everyone you meet when you are out and about. As with all networking, you never know who will see your posts and who people know. Once you become a regular in people's feeds, they will look to see what you do and probably connect with you.

Marketing comes before sales so your strategy should include being more visible, going where your target audience are and engaging with as many people as possible. The more people see you, the more they will be curious to see what you are doing.

The key to all this is to keep that bigger picture in your head. Whenever you are offered a new opportunity, think about whether it takes you closer to your goal or not. If it does, then great; if it doesn't, then decline and move on. Every small step you take in the right direction will get you closer to where you want to be.

Businesses should be spending approximately 20 per cent of their time on strategy. That sounds a lot for many business owners but the profit is in the strategy, joint ventures and collaborations. Spending time in this area of your business and working out exactly what you want and how you are going to get there will pay off in the long term.

A business plan is a fantastic tool to keep you on track. Plan what you want to achieve, set targets and then monitor your performance to see if you are on track. If you are, that's fantastic. If you aren't quite achieving what you want, have a look at where things are going astray and focus on that area.

Knowledge is key. The more you know about your business and how it's performing, the more opportunity you have to change your strategy in order to get to the place you want to be. Ignoring the numbers, not focusing on strategy are all recipes for disaster and one of the reasons why businesses fail or don't achieve their potential.

Plan your journey and achieve your goals!

***Sally Marshall***

Every dream starts with a vision. The only difference is a dream is something and a vision does something. A dream is a place to be and a vision is a place to go. So how do you make that vision into reality? My vision a few years ago was to step out on stage and win my PRO card for my first body building competition. This is not something that just happened overnight, I had to work for it! I spent my days weight training, doing long hours of cardio, prepping, cooking and eating 6 meals a day as well as training my PT clients and working on my business. The one question I used to get asked by my friends was, "How do you fit it all in?" My answer to that is we all have the same 24 hours in a day it is just how we decide to use it.

This is when you ask yourself, "what is my why?" "Why am I doing this?" "Why is this important to me?" When you find your why you will find your purpose. It is one of life's greatest joys to wake up every morning with a clear sense of why that day matters. After all, if your business doesn't meet your personal goals, you probably won't be happy waking up each morning and trying to make the business a success. Define what it is that makes you get up every morning.

Now I believe that if you're reading this you already have a purpose. Whether your purpose involves property, marketing, accountancy or fitness we are all in it for the same reason. Our journeys may be different but our destination is the same. The destination to success.

In order to achieve that success it's very important that you realise the significance and importance of goal setting and apply this knowledge in your business. Goals are what take us forward in life and give us purpose. They are the first steps to every journey we take and are also our last. When setting your goals you need to be crystal clear with your end goal. For me my end goal was getting my PRO card, which is a pretty big goal for a first time competitor! It just meant that in order for that to happen I had to break that goal down into smaller goals in order to get there.

One of the biggest mistakes I see in goal setting is wanting to run before you can walk. Now don't get me wrong I am sometimes a victim of this! And most people in my generation are. They all have the *"I've got to have this right now"* mindset. Technology is growing so rapidly and it has made us dependent on the idea of always being connected. Anything we want from online shopping to communication are all a click away, every day. With the touch of a button we are connected to anything you could possibly want. So it's easy to understand why some people start a business and fail within their first year.

Growing a business takes time! So break those big goals down into more manageable smaller goals. This also allows you to celebrate each small goal, and keep your enthusiasm high, instead of risking frustration waiting to achieve one big goal. The best part is you are no longer relying on a super high level of motivation to keep yourself committed. The simpler the goal, the less motivation it requires to achieve it. "Never underestimate the power of simplicity".

## TREAT YOUR BUSINESS AS IF YOU WERE GOING ON HOLIDAY!

From my own experience I find that when I don't have goals in place my business comes to a standstill, my tasks are all over the place and I don't feel like I'm moving forward. If you fail to plan, you plan to fail. If you really want to make a success of your business, it's important to define your business goals before you get started.

Now let's use going on holiday as an example. You wouldn't book a holiday and not turn up to the airport on time? Forget your passport or not sort out your travel money would you? Of course not! From the moment you book that holiday you make sure everything that follows after it is planned out accordingly so you make your flight on time! So why would you not follow the same process within your business?

Having goals in place gives me a target to aim towards, a sense of direction. It allows me to focus on a goal rather than waste my energy on tasks that are not important, which allows me to hit my targets and reach my goals on time. How else would I manage to eat 6 meals a day! I tell you that requires a lot of planning! From a business point of view, when I first started, I had so many things I wanted to do but just did not have a clue where to start.

Once I began to research my industry and brain storm some ideas it was then just a case of doing it. Being a 2 person business the amount of work we had to do seemed daunting! All I used to think to myself was, "how are we ever going to fit all this in ?" This was due to the fact we had no goals in place. The one thing you do not want to do is start doubting yourself. The one thing you do want to do is have a word with yourself.

## SET TIMEBOUND GOALS!

Give some time to yourself to really think of what it is you REALLY want to achieve. Don't just think of this, write it down! I personally choose to have all my goals and business plans written up on sticky white board sheets in my living room so I can see it every day. Maybe you would prefer to have yours in a notepad or on your phone or laptop. Writing down our goals increases our chances of actually sticking to them.

My tip for you is, rather than starting from the start, start from the end and work your way back. This will make your goal setting so much easier. Break your goals down into years, months and weeks.

I personally give myself ten, five, three and one year goals. Then I break it down into six months and one month goals. Starting back gives you a clear vision of what you need to do in order to get there. Now being a busy business owner I can appreciate that staying on track with your goals can be tricky and somewhat overwhelming, so find yourself someone to be accountable to.

## GET YOURSELF SOME ACCOUNTABILITY!

Accountability groups or partners are steadfast motivators. There will be days when your motivation and mental strength will be tested and that passion you once felt might feel like it's starting to vanish. It's on these days that your accountability group will be your biggest up lifter and remind you why you do what you do in the first place. They help keep your goals in sight as you work to make them become a reality.

I attend a group once a month where we set each other realistic yet challenging goals that will push our business further. As an entrepreneur, it's exciting to go it alone and create something on your own. However, the reality is that, while you have a great idea, you may not know exactly what you should be doing with your business but someone else will.

One of the greatest benefits I find, being part of an accountability group, is the feeling that you will never walk your journey alone. There will always be someone to help motivate you and keep you on track. Working towards your goal becomes a team effort and, if you fail, you won't just be letting yourself down but the rest of the group too. My advice for you when searching for a group is to find one that will challenge you. Seek out someone you admire to help you reach higher heights.

I am a strong believer that what you put in is what you get out. So if you're putting in minimal effort when it comes to achieving your goals you will get minimal results. If you put in maximum effort you will get maximum results.

There's a book I suggest you should read called " The 10 X Rule" by Grant Cardone. He explains this theory and describes the one thing that ensures a person creates extraordinary success. It's nothing to do with genes, luck or connections. It's a lot more to do with thinking big and taking action. Some people dream of success whilst others wake up and work hard for it. Don't be 'some people'! How will you choose to spend your 24 hours?

*Emily Hackett*

# 3 *YOU*

*If you take you or the product out of a business all businesses are the same. They all have the same bits that make them work, however, the thing that will make a difference is YOU! Attitude is contagious and if your attitude is poor then the likelihood is your business will be struggling. Have a look at you and your beliefs about life, money, leadership, scarcity and abundance. Remember, everything is cause and effect, you can't plant bananas and pick cucumbers!* **Ash**

As I see it, (from the perspective of a small business owner myself), the problem in relation to self - development that most business owners face, is their lack of awareness around their skill set. Some think they know it all and carry on with this misconception drawn heavily over their eyes and ears, whilst others lack self-confidence and belief.

They don't feel investing in themselves will be worth it. Or it's a simple truth that they spend so much time looking at the business they forget to work on and themselves, or take action on the knowledge they have learned.

Either way, as a business owner, you can be seemingly blind to the benefits that changing yourself can bring to your personal and business life. It can be challenging to see yourself as an asset that needs attention to fulfil true potential and reap the rewards. You're often "too busy" to stop and take stock.

Only when you hit a brick wall, face a really tough challenge, realise your skillset deficit, do you consider taking the pathway to YOU. Ask yourself this question, "how can you expect anyone else to invest in you, your products, your services, your business, if you don't value yourself enough to invest in YOU first?"

Adopting the mindset to be a lifelong learner, and being honest enough to admit you don't know it all, is the leap of faith we all need to take. This takes an understanding of our weaknesses and strengths. That understanding, that awareness, is the precursor to change. The willingness to play the game to win, to be the best version of you, and take action on what you then seek to learn.

In most part due to bad habits, and ingrained ways of doing things that were long since questioned, we are getting the results we deserve because they are the result of our current actions and patterns of behaviour. Excuses and justification fight to protect our current practices and we are caught in a "rinse and repeat" cycle. Lack of awareness hides the warning signals that change in you is necessary for growth.

My personal journey with self-development picks up on the self-confidence issue, forgetting to focus on me and not taking action on my knowledge.

I've always loved learning and trying to make a better me. My thirst for information is strong. Whilst many people stop learning once their education path finished, I've never done that. What I did though, was to learn more and more and yet not have the confidence or support to put that knowledge into action for myself and my business.

My belief system was damaged, (for various reasons), and I didn't feel my knowledge was valuable or valued in the business. Now I'm no different to many business owners – we all face challenges in our lives and sometimes we allow them to dent our confidence to "have a go".

Fear of failure plagues us and handbrakes our progress, and consequently our success.

My levels of frustration grew to almost breaking point. I knew what needed to be done but didn't do it! How mad is that? Accumulating relevant and business changing skills and not implementing them in your own business!

I was paralysed in my own business but great at spotting what my friends needed to do in their businesses, coming up with plenty of ideas for them. In fact I had the ideas for my own business in an "ideas box" and documented in a book too, but that's where most of them languished.

Instead of action, I know recognise that I made excuses and played the "blame game", and all the time the frustration levels grew and my self-anger was fuelled. Now it makes me sound as if I did nothing – not so. I did stuff but it was mostly unplanned and rarely consistent.

The other problem I faced with developing myself was being hampered by "perfectionism". Until experiencing the Millionaires Mindset course, I'd always thought perfectionism was a positive trait – wanting to get stuff just right had been drilled into me at school. I've since learnt that perfectionism is procrastination disguised in utopian costume! It handcuffs you and holds you back.

So I'd suggest to any of you reading this, who describes themselves as a perfectionist, to really think about it. Think how many times, "not being able to get it perfect", has stopped you from getting something started. As Ash Lawrence will tell you, "Just get it going!"

As Mahatma Gandhi said, *"You must be the change you wish to see in the world"*, and *"Live as if you were to die tomorrow. Learn as if you were to live forever."*

I'm no revered expert but I can share my learnings and journey with you, and hope it might strike a chord with some of you. It may encourage you to start or restart your journey about YOU.

Embrace change in yourself, have courage to fail, aim to inspire those around you, and engage in life fully. Challenge yourself to open your mind to everything being possible until it proves to be otherwise. After all, the difference between good and great lies in the quality of your thinking, which in turn relates to the quality of your self-development.

Action is the cure and it is certainly proving to be so for me. As Deborah Jones, another contributor to this book, said at a recent **Entrepreneurs Business Club** meeting, action eases anxiety, and I wholeheartedly agree. Taking some action is better than just "intending" to do something which really means you're not committed to doing it at all! Does that resonate with any of you reading this?

Just get it going and travel from your current situation, your current practices, to a better one and then onto the best outcome.

To move your business forward, as all businesses must to succeed, I urge you to move YOURSELF forward first. Your business will follow as soon as you learn the skills, especially the mindset skills, and USE them.

I can only suggest what is helping me; take responsibility for yourself, your life, your choices and your attitude. Take a shortcut and learn from others who've been there, done it and then written the book – read that book!

Revisit your beliefs and challenge them, and retrain your brain to replace the old bad habits with new levels of thinking and cultivate exciting new habits for your best YOU! Let go to leap forward.

I'd be a total hypocrite if I wasn't challenging myself to do all the things I've just mentioned. So, as I don't intend to add hypocrisy to my negative traits, I can confirm that I am having a go at all of it – remember what I've already said – moving from now to better to best!

As I reached a point of absolute frustration and confusion in my own business I knew change was vital. I looked for courses and mentors that could help me out and I stumbled across Ash Lawrence and the Millionaires Mindset course.

"The pain of the same was greater than the pain of change"– if you don't quite get this phrase just yet, contact Ash #FlipFlopPsycho, and he'll explain it far better than me!

After experiencing the 2 hour taster course I knew I had to find the time and invest the money in myself to do the full years course.

I started that course in April 2016, and my business partner, (also my husband), joined the course 3 months later when he realised the value it had to offer both of us and our business. I haven't thought in the same way since and I don't think I ever will. And that's a good thing!

I've learned loads but more importantly I now do my level best to take action on my newfound knowledge, and one of the key phrases Ash repeats is "Say what you do, do what you say" and "Do It Now" (DIN).

I have embraced the teachings, left my set of beliefs outside the meeting room every time and loved the course. Now I'm enrolled on the Entrepreneurs Business Club, so I can learn more and be held accountable to take action.

There's much work in progress for me. I don't presume to know it all. In fact I adopt the attitude that I don't know enough and so I'm ready to absorb as much as I can from other people. Like I said before I'm no revered expert.

Personally, I've committed to daily exercise, meditation and reading. I'm practicing a better positive mental attitude.

Now it may sound weird to some of you at the moment, but now I've also adopted a mantra I say to myself every day, several times a day – sometimes quietly and sometimes as loud as I dare, which I share below-

*"I expand with love, happiness and success every day, as I inspire those around me to do the same".*

I learned about mantras and their power whilst listening to one of the many audiobooks I have on my phone now thanks to the new way I think and act on self-development – it's part of my every day routine. I dare you to try it for a week and see if it makes a difference. Let me know how you get on.

On a business level, I've adopted so many changes covering systems & processes, sales, marketing, lead generation, customer service and on it goes!

It's not "perfect", but then again I'm not looking for perfection any more. That's a lesson well learned.

I'm going to give stuff a try! What's the worst that can happen? If it goes right, great. If it goes wrong, I've learned something!

Doing the worst thing first is still a tough ask but at least I'm aware of the need to achieve this and continue to work at it. I just remember that awareness precedes change (as I've said before!).

Thanks to building an abundance mentality I'm seeing new possibilities and business opportunities, and my business has won some bigger clients as a result. More networking, more social media, (although I've still got L plates, or maybe with optimistic enthusiasm, P plates still firmly fixed on my business bonnet), more joint ventures and collaboration - more more more…

**Life is for living – get up, get out and get going!**

*Rachel Cowell*

*"To have more than you've got, become more than you are"*

What you become in life is infinitely more important than anything you might get. Being true to yourself in all factors of your life is what will determine your future success. Unfortunately most people just focus on what they will get out of a situation rather than what they will become from it. What you become directly influences what you get. Think of it this way: most of what you have today, you have attracted by becoming the person you are today.

I remember back to when I was at university. I was a dance student with a very negative mindset and approach to life. I found that each day felt like a struggle, I lacked motivation and I generally wasn't happy with my life. I had this vision in the back of my mind that my future would hold success. I just don't think I realised that it was down to me to create that success.

My days were spent blaming others for all the negative events that were happening in my life until I discovered that the only person that can change your circumstances is you. I was focusing more on, "why am I not getting what I want?", rather than, "what can I do to become who I want?"

The person I once was, is gone and never to be seen again! Over the last 2 years I have been lucky to meet some inspirational people that have changed my life for the better. I have completely changed my mindset. I have been able to grow in all aspects of my life, especially in my business, and it was simply through focusing on personal development.

Once you have turned all your attention to, "what can I do to be better?", the "getting what you want" part will come naturally. It might not be an immediate result, however the journey you will take getting there will make you into a better person.

Now I'm not going to lie and say personal development is easy, it's not. It's a challenge! But if everything in life was just handed to you then how will you ever learn to grow? We don't improve when things are easy. We improve when we are faced with challenges and that's what life is all about.

*"Challenges are what makes life interesting and overcoming them is what makes life meaningful!"*

Life is all about creating and learning new skills. Having inspiration is great but inspiration must lead to discipline. It's one thing to say your motivated but how motivated are you to find time to do a new course, read a book and take classes on a regular basis.

Self-development is not something you can just do as a one off,

It's all about creating and putting into place the foundations and building blocks for future. Making positive changes will allow you to become the best possible version of yourself and live the best life experience possible. Spend more time developing as a person rather than a business owner/ manager.

*"Change your thoughts and you change your world" Wayne Dyer*

So how can you continue to develop in your business? Well firstly, it starts with self-improvement and making measurable progress . Your self-improvement journey should involve gathering new knowledge and understanding as well as learning from your failures and mistakes. This will then allow you to be wiser, better and stronger. However, in order to do that, you must create new habits. New habits don't come easily but they can be developed.

This requires a new way of thinking and going against what you subconsciously tell yourself on a day to day basis. It's called changing your belief systems.

Now it's pretty simple when you think about it. All you have to do is look at who you are, where you have come from and how you wish to move forward. However the secret is to believe in your potential and know your value.. now that's the hard part.

Let's use selling a product as an example. You will say out loud, "I really hope I sell this", even though subconsciously you are thinking "I don't think this will sell". Your words may sound optimistic but they don't bring the results you want. If your subconscious is putting out doubt how can it manifest what you actually want?

From my own experience I remember back to a time when I wanted to get sponsored by a clothing brand. Now being a fitness model there is so much competition out there. All I kept thinking to myself was "why will they pick me out of everyone out there?" I didn't have a lot of followers compared to most of the other models but what I didn't realise, at that time, was that wasn't important.

A mentor and good friend of mine said to me, "what makes you any different to them?" And the answer was nothing. All that was different was my beliefs. They believed that they were good enough to get sponsored and I didn't, and all that comes down to is how we value ourselves.

By Entrepreneurs for Entrepreneurs!

I am now proudly sponsored by a gym clothing brand simply by changing my beliefs. Your mind is a powerful tool and if you fill it with positive thoughts your life will change.

"Life isn't about finding yourself it's about creating yourself". In today's world we have it so easy! So easy that you can access almost anything online. Gone are the days when we had to sit for hours in the library looking through books, or break the budget to take courses. I built up my whole social media business based on video tutorials that I accessed through YouTube.

Most people think that self-development is taking yourself off on a weekend course but actually nowadays you can learn almost anything off the internet. Just remember, anyone can sit down and watch a video. However, it's not the information it's the implementation.

I appreciate that finding time whilst running a business can be difficult but not impossible! There should always be time for self-improvement otherwise how can you keep on improving your services and products. Now I'm not a book reader myself, I find it really hard to sit down and read. One because my time is limited and two I find it hard to read from a black and white sheet of paper. Instead I use my time wisely and so when I'm on a long journey I will listen to audio books. Audio books are amazing as you can download the app to your phone and hook it up to the Bluetooth in your car. So now there's no excuses.

There is always room for self-expansion and growth. Many people shy away from the idea of personal development. It seems that the idea of becoming a better person and living a happier life is seen as silly and a waste of time. Apparently watching EastEnders and Game Of Thrones is a much better way to spend your time but on a serious note which one is going to make a bigger impact on your life?

No matter what type of person you are, ANYONE can and will benefit from working on themselves. See yourself as a work in progress. If you are an entrepreneur, which I gather you are if you're reading this book, then I suggest you devote time to bettering yourself. Take into account everything I've already spoken about as you'll most likely need to make some changes to your belief systems, as well as how you think and act.

Take a look at some of the most successful entrepreneurs of our life time. How do you think they built their success? Those who go on to be successful and achieve great things have a lifelong drive and relentless work ethic. Time spent on yourself is the greatest investment you can make.

Always remember "Competition is simply being better than the person you were yesterday".

*Emily Hackett*

# 4 *S*TAND OUT

*Very few people in the business world have a completely unique product or service. We are all competing with each other in a flooded market. The question is how do we stand out in that very full pond? Most people try to distinguish themselves by price and be cheaper than the next man. This, in my opinion, is the path to bankruptcy as all that will happen is a price war.*

*We have to fix a place in the client's mind so that they remember us and then want to buy or product or service. If I said to you "You can't get quicker than a \*\*\*\* \*\*\* \*\*\*\*\*\*" how would you complete that sentence? Probably with "Kwik Fit fitter!" Now, do you really believe that Kwik Fit fitters are faster than any other tyre or exhaust fitter? Of course not. However, Kwik Fit have fixed a place in your mind.*

*This happens everywhere in business and once you start looking you will see it in virtually all corporate businesses. Your mission is to stand out like this in your business so that people remember you for all of the right reasons!* **Ash**

One of the main things that most businesses struggle with is, how do you get noticed in your industry's marketplace? What will make you stand out and different from your competitors? You can focus on one of four things; product, market, service or price.

Having learnt this for my business, I can now recognize those businesses that really aren't getting this right, at all, as well as companies who have got it right! For me, John Lewis has this spot on. They market to a high end customer. Their products are not for everyone, or more specifically, their price point may not be.

What I will say about their products is they are really good quality and great value for money, despite their price being four times the price for a similar item, that say B&Q would sell. Also, they always give longer warranties compared to most other places I know. This combination is designed to be attractive to a particular customer type, that typically uses their stores.

If the four (product, market, service and price) are not balanced correctly then all could go belly up. I used to sell a lot of different products with a very low profit in them and not sell enough to make any money. I was also trying to sell to anyone and everyone.

In my opinion, this was me being similar to Aldi. Not that there is anything wrong with this, if you're selling enough items, and you have the customer base that this appeals to and you can sell enough. The issues I had with this was that I couldn't keep up with the demands of the customer whilst maintaining the high level of service I offer. The low profit margin meant I couldn't afford to hire enough staff to keep up with such demand.

If I bought cheaper products that had no quality in them I would get a failure rate and returns. These were not the products I wanted to sell nor did I want customers that kept bartering on my price even though it was already cheaper than other internet stores.

Of course, I would be earning more profit but creating a load more work and still getting unhappy customers. So, as you can see all four; product, market, service and price, need to be right for the market position you want to hold. Get this right and you will; make enough profit to be able to hire the staff you require, keep your clients happy and returning to you no matter your price and then this will help you position your company or yourself where you want to be.

Soon I realised that if you take just one product that is good and find the right customer that really trusts your company values they will pay a very fair price for the item you are selling without looking for a better price elsewhere. This is like the customers Waitrose have. They are prepared to pay a higher price for the same branded products that Asda sell at a cheaper price.

The question is how can one outlet charge much higher than the other? Charging a premium price for the same product? This may well be due to the different customer service and experience you get from one to the other. These are powerful tools in setting the position a company takes in the mind of the consumer.

One of my biggest business challenges came after starting my business in 1998, and positioning myself as a computer repair / installation engineer in the middle of Docklands London. This was too generic in terms of positioning and didn't differentiate me as an expert above all the many engineers, who had far less experience and expertise.

I had to do something very special to continue to earn the money I had been used to, at the price I wanted to charge.

There were no viruses and malware as experienced now, very little remote support functionality, and cybercrime had not been heard of!

I was living in London and advertising in an area where we had 2-5 calls a day from the "big large yellow book" that was delivered to every business and house. The IT industry was not swamped with many specialised companies that knew how to fix computer software, hardware and network cabling faults or how to do computer system installations.

I then moved to Kent due to personal relationship changes – namely marriage! I still continued to work out of London until I built a customer base in Kent. This created a completely new set of problems in advertising and finding how and where to market my business.

Whilst waiting for an advert to be put in Yellow Pages and the Thomson Local, I decided to start reselling at computer fairs all over Kent. Selling to all and sundry with all types of IT products that made some money. It didn't really make the money I needed to as it was just mass selling to a customer base that was purely based around cheap pricing, which requires volume sales and is not based on quality of product or good service. Having said that, it did introduce me to several very large and good quality returning customers, which I'm proud to service to this day.

In 2003, I was introduced to networking in the form of business breakfast meetings. I'd like to take this opportunity to thank Gary Guillon of Timemaker Systems, a web design company, for the initial introduction to networking. Over the years I have built amazing relationships with many other businesses through networking, such as Grace Kelly of 21st Century Flooring. These relationships are ongoing and we help promote each other's businesses wherever appropriate.

At those breakfast meetings, I would stand up and deliver my 60 seconds talk as a computer repair man, who could fix and install computers etcetera without clearly positioning myself in people's minds.

We then started to see more and more computer viruses attacking workstations and file servers. This led me to a great opportunity with a major anti-virus company in 2005 that I found at a show held at the NEC, Birmingham. *F-secure* were looking for partner resellers for their software protection. What a fantastic opportunity! We'd been selling software protection from companies like Norton and AVG, which in my opinion where never that great, but they were the best of their kind at the time.

After partnering with *F-secure* , their product opened my eyes to the level of criminal activity on the internet. This inspired me to really get to grips with the product and become an expert in the industry. Soon I was a silver partner of *F-secure*, and started to build my customer base. I am now a gold partner!

It was not until 2013 when the Millionaire Mindset course opened my eyes to how I could position my business and make me stand out and be remembered.

Taking the supermarkets as an example of positioning again, you can see how they have each positioned themselves to appeal to, and indeed attract, a specific customer type. What the consumer ranks important will determine where they see each supermarket in their mind. Aldi and Asda will have a different customer profile to Waitrose and M & S, (by design!).

I wanted to be positioned like Waitrose and Marks and Spencer. As a small business I felt I would be unable to service many customers cheaply, like the Aldi and Lidl's of this world. So I'd need the higher paying client that wanted me to "pack their shopping", and take full care of them and give them, not only a service they could rely on, but an experience they would be happy paying a premium price for.

Now I had decided on the position and client I wanted. My next step was to make Verbo Computers stand out from other computer companies. We did this with the help of the award-winning *F-secure* products we have partnered up with. Products that we ourselves, believed in, and that reinforced our positioning as "the best".

By aligning my business with the best products, and having expert knowledge and standout service levels, I have built on the "know, like, trust" model and created a "stand out" position in the market.

I'll give you an example of how easy it is now to present my business in a networking situation thanks to the clarity I have in my business positioning.

I have a 60 second "elevator" speech where I use a condom to illustrate protection, security and back up for your IT. Not just any condom, but the bestselling quality protection, Durex. It all relates to quality, premium product and service, and the importance of IT security, safety and back up! As you can imagine, this truly started to get me remembered, and became a talking piece about what I did in the computer world for my clients. I never needed to talk about other products we sell or our services.

Once we became a very trusted source to protect your I.T devices, the remote support and other products sold itself making it very easy to grow our business.

We then added other products that fitted around the protection for all I.T. devices. I developed the analogy further with the introduction of a small branded box, (made by a small crafting company). It was a simple box that housed my pack of 3 Durex in – well I.T protection comes in three's; cyber security, privacy and back up.

These 3 created another great package or bundle of services that our company offer which has proven successful in sales.

Not only am I confident in presenting my services in this way, I have developed other "products" as a platform to demonstrate I'm a trusted expert in my field. This in itself affirms my positioning. I now hold monthly free events where I talk about specific IT issues -educational for the audience and a great tool to position me in the prospects mind as the "go to" IT company. It also acts as an advertorial for my portfolio of IT products and services.

The great news about all these products is that I have streamlined and cash-flowed my business at the same time. Many of the products I've chosen to offer are yearly subscription products, which means they bring in predictable residual income on an annual or now monthly basis. After all, if Microsoft can do it, why not Verbo Computers!

Sort your positioning, and it will sort your profit!

***Chris Verbiest***

We had excitement, we had drive, and we had a fair bit of knowledge within our industry when we launched our business, Clockwork Moggy. Our main problems were cash flow, a very common one for start-ups, and finding a gap in the saturated market that is graphic and web design. Something we never considered until later in our business journey mindset.

We frequently asked ourselves questions like:

"What are we going to do that is different to everyone else?"

"How are we planning to achieve the difference?"

"What answers are we going to have for people when they ask the big question

"What makes us different?"

"How are we going to stand out from the massive amount of competition?

We needed to work out what products and services we were going to offer, our price range, who we were going to sell our services to, and how we were going to promote our business to effectively represent our brand. Money was tight. In the first few months after setting up, Mac computers cost a lot!

We were so quick to try and make our money back from our investment, that we made the mistake of rushing through the positioning process without any real strategy on the who's, what's, why's and when's and what we wanted to achieve.

Out of excitement and panic, we did make a few mistakes. Building a really quick website with no real goal in mind. We didn't consider a specific target market, and we were very focused on just accepting projects from anyone to make our money back and build up our portfolio.

We didn't want to be known as a 'cheap' design company although we did lower prices on occasions to get people through the door and get the client base rolling. I was worried! We started our business during the recession, I had just handed in my notice at work (magazine design) and Neil took redundancy from his previous job so there was no back-up, a real sink or swim situation. Thankfully however we did take time to think about our company name and brand identity.

We wanted to have a quirky brand that suggested that we're different, efficient and approachable creative thinkers. We knew how important it is to get the logo right from the start, and to make a good first impression when prospective clients started to identify with our brand. More on this later.

Another problem we faced was that we had no prior experience. This was the first time either of us had run a business. We had qualifications coming out of the wazoo, we had creativity and plenty of excitement and drive, but no real idea on how to run a business, and especially not on how to properly position ourselves. So our journey started with trial and error.

We were guessed and tried different ways to make money. To build our illustration portfolio, we made digital artwork and sold it at Greenwich Market. We didn't know at the time but this was definitely the wrong market for us, tourists that wanted cheap gifts or locals on an impulse buy.

Not the type of client that would appreciate the hours or skill that had gone into each piece or pay the price tag on them. So we stopped doing what wasn't working.

I was still designing a magazine and had the odd small jobs coming in and Neil had a very sparse list of websites. The results were reflecting the planning that we had put in. We knew something had to change or we weren't going to last long as a business, especially not through a recession.

We started making changes and later learned that there was a whole new world out there. People that could help young entrepreneurs and startup businesses. We came across a company, The Kent Foundation, who did exactly that. They give free advice to young entrepreneurs to help them start out in business.

We booked a meeting with them and as a result found an amazing mentor who we met up with once a month to go through our plans and ideas and generally what we had done through the month. It was really helpful and a good starting place for us to recognise that much more planning and vision was needed. So we went back to the drawing board and devised a plan of action with real goals in mind.

The Kent Foundation also introduced us to business exhibitions and networking, a very different world to the small magazine design business I had worked with before. Now we were on track. We had written our business plan and started putting things in place to achieve our goals.

We worked out our pricing, the exact services we were offering and the ideal client that we wanted to work with, and the thoughts and feelings we wanted people to have when they heard about us.

By Entrepreneurs for Entrepreneurs!

Despite knowing what we needed to do we still found things difficult at this stage. I suffered with anxiety, rejected public speaking opportunities, producing video was a no no, and even standing up for 60 seconds at the beginning of a networking event would terrify me. I've always loved doing what I do, but having the confidence to express that and believing that I was good enough had always been a niggle in the back of my mind. I spent too much time comparing our business to other companies and myself to other designers.

Once again we needed help. This time from someone who understands and teaches business mindset so we could achieve our goals and become the successful company we wanted to be.

So another journey began on the Millionaire Mindset course by Ash Lawrence. Every detail of the business was looked at and revised. From general every day systems and processes to re-pricing, tweaking every aspect of the business that our clients were coming into contact with, and, of course, repositioning.

We had already established a good reputation by this point and a good number of our clients were coming to us through recommendations (a great sign you're doing something right). We wanted to be recognised as a trustworthy and unique design company that offered something that little bit different.

Whilst going through the running of the business with a fine tooth comb with the Millionaire Mindset course, we were also assigned a 'buddy' for the month. We would meet up with another member of the course to discuss our goals and our progress in between our monthly course meet-ups.

The accountability worked really well for us as work can sometimes take over and it's easy to spend all of your time working rather than spending time on your business.

Setting goals for your business is a great tactic for any business. Whether that's working out your ideal client, price changes, new products/services or even something in your personal life that needed to be resolved to enable you to clearly focus on what needs to be done in your business.

Business was on the up again and more of our ideal clients were naturally coming to us.

We redesigned our website making sure it was doing everything we tell our clients to do, and redesigned our marketing material and how we promoted our services. We networked more often. I started to tackle the anxiety of public speaking by putting on presentations and workshops and we tweaked our systems and processes for everything we were doing. From how we run client meetings to revising each stage of our services ran smoothly.

By making these changes our reputation and client base grew. We were becoming the 'go to' company for web design and branding. We even had a waiting list of companies willing to wait around 5 months to work with us.

It's a great feeling when people you've never met before know you through your good reputation. As well as putting a smile on our faces, we also recognised that our reputation afforded us the opportunity to hire another pair of hands and to offer a new service.

By Entrepreneurs for Entrepreneurs!

We expanded into SEO and online marketing services. As we were already a trustworthy company, this new service gained us a new client in the first few days of launching!

With any business that's doing well it will naturally begin to grow, and knowing how to deal with growth may require looking into positioning again. You have to ask yourself, "are we positioned correctly for the potentially larger clients coming in?", "can we meet their higher demands and expectations?" In most cases you'll find that your business will tell you which route to take.

A business is like an animal over time - ever evolving, ever changing. Technology changes, the way people buy things and interact with your brand changes. It's so important to stay on top of these changes or be left behind.

*"It is not the strongest or the most intelligent who will survive but those who can best manage change."*
--Charles Darwin

For us, our new service and overall business growth triggered changes in our business as a whole. The need for strong brand identity spiked as companies started to realise the power of a strong brand and identity. I had the workload covered but in order to add value to our clients I tweaked the presentation and customer experience part of the service.

We tweaked our web design service to focus on the marketing of the site. Something we had always done but never showcased before. This led directly into our new online marketing service.

The last thing we needed to nail down within the business was deciding on what our USP was, our unique selling point. It's tough, really tough, when you start thinking about it. There's so much competition out there. We had to ask ourselves what we could offer that no one else could. We didn't know, so we spoke to other businesses and listened to our existing clients. We asked them what problems they had experienced in the past and how we could resolve them?

We heard that many other design companies had over promised and under delivered, and often deadlines were being put back or in some cases not being met at all with contracts cancelled. Thankfully, we were known for getting the job done well and on time. We had found our USP. We re-positioned ourselves once again with our new company motto: *"On time every time, like clockwork"* and moved from our home office to a lovely, creative professional office space banishing the stigmas that come from working from home.

We have established trust from our clients. We have answered their 'needs, wants and concerns' and provide a service that's in high demand for our sector. The results speak for themselves and our reputation is the one we set out for.

***Carrie Stay***

Positioning is a tricky strategy to get spot on, and this fact alone, discourages business owners from dealing with this strategy in a timely fashion. Often they don't do it at the start of their business and simply fall into a position.

Also, even when business owners consider positioning in their marketing mix, they start in the wrong place. Working on the solution without thinking through the problem. Business owners haven't asked themselves some key questions to explore the market position they should take, and then plan the strategy to obtain it. They just start and hope positioning will naturally take effect.

Positioning as a marketing tool is difficult. History is littered with many big companies, with vastly more resources than most of us, who have fallen foul of the latest marketing fad.

Business owners look in the wrong direction too.

What I mean is they view the positioning from within their business – an inside out approach. So they look at their business, their products and services from their own stand point and not from the prospects perspective. There's an old saying about, "walking a mile in another person's shoes ", to truly understand someone and this is certainly true for positioning. We, as business owners, all need to start walking in the prospects and customers shoes, or more accurately thinking as they think and living inside their mind space.

Lastly, business owners trip up with positioning because they lack a long- term vision and acceptance of change. They have not planned their business forward to 1, 3, 5 and 10 years.

As Al Ries, author of "Positioning" remarks-

*"Change is a wave on the ocean of time. Short- term, the waves cause agitation and confusion. Long-term, the underlying currents are more significant. To cope with change, you have to take a long-range point of view. To determine your basic business and stick to it."*

Inadequate or inaccurate positioning creates fog in the consumers mind.

Finding our "X-factor" has been an unanswered question for too long.

At JUSTSO, we feel our brand is strong in terms of visual representation and brand consistency. People always seem to remember our logo and straplines, and being remembered is a great start to being used. However, since developing our services from just branded clothing with embroidery, (hence JUSTSO), to all things branded (clothing branding, promotional items, merchandise platforms and more), we are looking to refine and focus our positioning within specific niches and targeted product zones.

We face this challenge as I write. You may therefore think that I'm not best placed as an authority on this subject, and you may well be right! However, facing this challenge now means I can share my journey. Awareness precedes change so perhaps reading this will raise your awareness, and support you to make changes in your business.

In an overcrowded market with multiple players, products and marketplaces, we lacked prospect focus and had a fixed viewpoint from inside our business. We saw our business and product positioning from our own perspective. We believed our USP, our X-factor was based

By Entrepreneurs for Entrepreneurs!

on our expertise, our "better than the rest" customer service, our consistent and superior brand treatment and decoration……..

In reality, these factors are what prospects, planning to purchase, would expect as standard! So our "stand outs" were standard!

We needed to focus on the client's perception and not the reality of the situation, and reverse engineer our thinking. A "fuzzy" long-term business vision, (and therefore strategy), hampered our planning, and planning your long-term vision is really the starting point to work back from. Building depth in the positioning to fix our core products and services in our prospects minds before going for line extensions and product growth.

Our challenge is to define the current market position we occupy and stand out from our many other competitors in terms that the customer relates to, and not just fits the way "we want to work".

We needed to create the right rung on the ladder that exists in prospects minds when they are rationalising their purchase choices. Organising our products and services to help customers build our position in their heads. Consumers, like chickens, want a pecking order that everyone knows and accepts.

The product explosion combined with the over-communicated society everyone operates within now, means that people simplify down to cope with the many options available to them. People will rank businesses and products in relation to each other. After all your brain has 3 ways to process information- it deletes, it distorts or it generalises.

To get your position along that ladder, business owners need to ask themselves several key questions to explore the challenge of positioning and creating stand out, before creating the solution.

Before we explore the questions that form the basis for delivering a "stand out" solution, it's probably useful to cement what positioning is-

*"Positioning is an organised system for finding a window in the mind"* (Al Ries – Positioning).

As the French say *"cherchez le creneau"* – look for the hole- in the market, in the product offering, in the service sector, the gap in the prospects mind.

So back to the questions that business owners should answer to begin a strong long-term positioning strategy that will float on the "ocean of change" (as mentioned at the start of this written conversation), and be elastic enough to stretch with the changing products and services on offer.

These questions apply equally to positioning a business, products or services, and positioning yourself. Business owners often forget their personal brand and how to position themselves congruently to their business (or career).

Where are you now?

What are you now?

Answer this from your prospects point of view, and not what you think. The context is always outside-in, from your clients side.

By Entrepreneurs for Entrepreneurs!

What position would you like to own?

Be honest and don't let your business ego, pride in your own business, your past behaviour and competitors get in the way. Identify an existing gap or create a new "gap" for yourselves.

Who are you up against?

Positioning should never be considered in isolation. We all need to research our competitors and work out where we can fit. Always be mindful that when customers use you, they have made a conscious choice. They want expectations to be met. They will see what they expect to see, and they will experience what they expect to experience. As businesses, we need to position our offerings with consumers expectations matched.

Have you taken a long term view? Have you reverse engineered your business strategy from there, working back to your current position, so you can define your basic stand out factor? Something I learned on the Millionaires Mindset course, called the G.R.O.W model, really helped me tackle our positioning strategy as well as many other business strategies. It goes like this;-

**G** is for Goals – Set your goals and check them off in terms of SMART criteria. Create the stepping stones that make up the journey to the ultimate goal (in this instance, your positioning goal).

**R** is for Reality – Where are you currently? Be honest! Don't justify anything, just give feedback on your current position.

**O** is for Options – What are your options to move from the current situation to the goal? Explore as many options as possible, with the mindset that everything is possible. Don't be blocked by past experience, financial constraints for this exercise. Simply push for more options and think outside the box. Answer the "what if….. " scenarios and push your thinking. Don't be handcuffed by concerns over finance, time, staffing levels etc. at this point – just open your mind to possibilities, and avoid the "but.." negative responses. Just explore, and then explore some more!

**W** is for What and When – get specific! Choose a specific option from the list of options you've explored in the step above, and then set a specific timescale.

Are you consistent and congruent?

People need a consistent message, look, feel and experience to build your product, service, business and personal positioning. This consistency should filter through all aspects of your business, and applies to your staff, systems and processes, presentations and pitches, your personal image, your service delivery, the language across all communication platforms and so forth. (Think Coca Cola, think Virgin)

Are you flexible?

Now I'm not referring to your physical flexibility obviously! Are you mentally flexible enough to leverage change and leverage the words you use to realistically position your business and trigger the meanings people will naturally attach to your products and verify their choices. Can you adapt your thinking to think as the consumer does, and not as you? If you only think as you've habitually done, then you'll only get what you've always got!

By Entrepreneurs for Entrepreneurs!

Creating "stand out", and positioning your business is an ongoing organic process. We have taken some steps already, but at the same time, we are continuing the journey in positioning our overall business effectively, as well as for our diverse range of products and services. We are looking at; developing specific niches, new service tiers, and new price levels to suit specific prospects, all of which support our core business positioning, and at the same time offer more customer service for our clients.

We have returned to the key influence for positioning – the "punter". Using data analysis, we have revisited customer databases, identified our "ideal" customers in both divisions of our business (branded clothing & promotional items) and formed a profile to position against so we attract more of the same.

At the same time, we have created a questionnaire which was sent to all customers, present and past, to capture their responses to key questions that reflect what's important and pertinent to purchase our products. What clients like, dislike, would like, where we sit in their heads, what we could improve, what's missing, what they want in the future.

This feedback has focused our attention on what stand out we can generate.

We have realised that we need to revisit our business vision and strategic planning for 3, 5, 10 years regularly, and reverse engineer to review our current position to our planned one. You don't know what you don't know and until we learn more from our prospects and clients we can't make changes.

We are actively building our credibility and social proof to reinforce our business "story" and develop the strength of our pitches. Developing attention grabbers, straplines and strengthening our communications via traditional and online channels.

Of course, we are concentrating on developing a deep and comprehensive product offering in the areas we've identified from our research, in our core business, before developing new growth strategies. In the Millionaires Mindset course, we learned about platform strategies and growth strategies. Each requires a different set of priorities to concentrate on.

Platform strategies basically mean you focus on doing the core things well and to near full capacity, using your existing infrastructure. You fill your "existing cup" up, and once you reach 70% capacity, you then start thinking about your growth strategies and tip your business into a "bigger" cup, and then work out ways to grow from there – filling your new bigger cup- more products, services, staff, machinery, more market infiltration…..

We have worked out that we need to concentrate on platform building strategies at the moment. Prior to this we had a slightly haphazard approach, as I'm sure many of you can relate to! Since completing the Millionaires Mindset course and now with the support of the EBC (**E**ntrepreneurs **B**usiness **C**lub), we are focusing on "filling our existing cup" before getting a bigger one out of the business cupboard!

Awareness of the importance to develop skills in creating the right "pitch" or "pitches", (also explored on the MMS course), has also provided greater focus in our business in general, because we now ask ourselves "what itch can we fix", "what pain can we take away" for the prospect.

Taking stock of our current situation and auditing our business through the lens of our potential and existing customers is helping us strengthen our positioning, and actively design the position we need to occupy as a business, rather than just waiting for it to happen!

Analysing our current customer base and lapsed customer base has given us new collateral to move forward with. "What gets measured gets changed" as Ash Lawrence frequently said on the MMS course! Better identifying our prospect profile means we're able to view all facets of our business through their eyes. It's an eye-opening process which I wholeheartedly recommend to all business owners! Too often we forget "why" we do something and this returns the focus. (I use that word so much now don't I, but that's because it's vital to achieving your goals!).

We have sacrificed some proposed product and service development for now, to concentrate on our core position. We don't want to create a "fog of confusion" to our prospects. You can't be all things to all people and at the same time have a strong position.

A.C.T – Analyse, Choose, Target for positioning strength. In other words, analyse your current market, pricing, customers, competition, products. Know where you are. Then choose your position, and target accordingly.

Our online positioning is gaining strength, (although it's still a challenge for me to commit more time to this activity), and better presence at networking events (armed with better pitch and presentation skills) means we have the opportunity to reinforce our business and build our profile in the minds of more people.

Networking works if you work it and as a business, we attend ABC Networks, BNI and Fore Business, to name a few.

There are always results to be achieved as we build content in our business – developing pricing structures and service packages that appeal to specific prospects, building a position in specific markets, and on it goes. I'm sure you have as many actions to be taken as we have. All businesses do. The critical factor is forming our positioning within the context of the prospect and consumer.

We are walking through our business in their footsteps. Good luck finding the footprints you need to follow, so you can achieve your best stand out, your best positioning, your best business.

*Rachel Cowell*

# 5 TEN OUT OF 10

*Having been in business for myself for two thirds of my life, I've seen a lot of businesses come and go and one of the main reasons for that is a poor lead generation process. When I first started the Millionaire Mindset program I was working with a group of 16 small business owners and we were discussing how you could make ten phone calls, get ten appointments and make ten sales... They all said it was improbable if not impossible to do that!*

*I gave them a copy of the Yellow Pages business directory, (shows you how long ago this was), and asked them to pick five random accountants. In front of them I called the five accountants and made five appointments from which I eventually made five sales. They were astonished; to me it was just having a tried and tested process!* **Ash**

When a consumer shows interest or makes an enquiry into products or services you provide, this is known as lead generation. These leads can be generated through a number of channels from online newsletter sign ups, through your website, SEO, networking, advertisements, referrals, social media etc. Done correctly, these tools can build your business nicely.

Tight budget - We all have big ideas for our businesses but with most big ideas comes big money! The last thing you want to do is spend the better part of your budget on an advertising campaign that isn't well executed .We had so many ideas and things we wanted to try. I guess we are pretty lucky as most of it i.e. website, SEO, branding, we can do ourselves, but we also had grand ideas for video marketing and needed the extra cash.

We saved what we could each month and carefully planned what the budget was going to go towards. In our case it was hiring a video specialist to further our brand online and make our ideas come to life.

We know the importance of video marketing and the stats behind YouTube etc so this was really important for our business. We were still on a tight budget, but with a little creative thinking and a great contact, we were able to get the finished product we were hoping for. Be a bit creative with your ideas. Great results can come from great ideas, not just a huge budget.

Social media is also a good way of getting your brand out there for free (if you have the time). LinkedIn has a lead generation feature. You can reach a wide target audience and your content can be easily shared. Customers that you didn't know existed can easily find you. Social media is also good for boosting your website's SEO.

If you get the social media presence right and build a strong following, they will be led to your website that's showcasing your company. Hopefully your website will be looking awesome and provide your customers with a great customer journey into your sales funnel. Of course, like anything else, you need to set the time aside to do it yourself if you are just starting out and budget is sparse. This can be quite time consuming since there are so many platforms to manage. With time and experience, you will begin to see which ones interact well with your prospective clients/customers and then you can focus on a few rather than all.

If you're looking for other free ways to promote your business, try blogging. This is a great way of answering popular questions/problems within your industry, and showing that you are competent and an expert within your field. This will naturally build trust and a following. Make sure you have a blog on your website as it will help greatly with your SEO and Google will see that you are regularly updating your website, and still alive and kicking.

If you don't feel confident with writing, there are people out there who will help you and are very reasonably priced.

Networking is also a great way to build relationships, reputation and generate leads face to face, adding that personal touch to your brand. You never know who you will meet and connect. What's more, you never know who they could potentially put you in contact with. It's about creating opportunities - not only to create new leads and more business but there might be other interests such as joint ventures and collaborations with people or businesses that share the same vision.

A popular saying – *"Your network is your net-worth and people really do buy from people - so get out there and get networking."*

Keeping up to date with tech and ways of building up interest in your product and services. Tech is constantly changing. There's always so much you can do and so much to be done when it comes to marketing your business. Keeping up to date with current trends, the changes in the way in which people buy, what Google likes and dislikes, knowing what your website should be doing, video marketing, social media and how to use it effectively etc etc. This can be a minefield for some, so I would suggest speaking with an expert. Devise a plan and strategy where these things work together for the best results.

Generating Leads Through SEO

From a study made in 2014 it was shown that direct traffic (traffic coming straight to your website by typing into the address bar of a browser), organic search (traffic coming for search engines such as Google), and web referrals ( traffic coming to your site through a link on somebody else's ), accounted for 93% of leads.

No matter how well you've organised your content, how great the offer is for your prospects, if there's no traffic to your page, you just won't get enough leads. And that's not just bad for your campaign, that's a waste of resources. Focus on optimizing your pages, either your official web page or your social media messages (posts, imagery – anything you post and share to promote your lead gen campaign). SEO is a major factor for a reason.

Since we offer SEO as a service, we can share some tips with you. SEO may seem like an overly complicated thing but a basic overview SEO is no more than 4 simple steps:

Target a keyword that your services fully represent and that your website is capable of ranking for. Create a well-optimised and well written piece of content about the target keyword that is better than what is currently ranking on the first page of Google for that keyword. It doesn't have to be long, perhaps no more than 300 words. Nor does it even have to overly sell your product but should present you as the font of knowledge for your industry. Thus selling your services for you.

Acquire relevant, authoritative backlinks and social media shares for the content. This is the hardest step but it is not impossible. Keep your social media profiles up to date to keep your followers engaged. That way, whenever you share your blog posts, you should get shares and likes more easily. Links are a little more difficult, but with some hard work they are achievable.

Lastly and probably most importantly make sure your website is pleasant. If users find it difficult to navigate, or if your site does not respond to mobile, they won't stay long enough to see the wonderfully written content you have created!

While it can be time consuming, SEO can provide you with leads that are more likely to convert than other channels, as they trust your knowledge and see you as the authority in your industry.

Website: Creating a customer journey - it is a term you may have heard web designers use. It is the pathway created from each page of your site to lead your users through the purchase funnel and hopefully lead them to convert to paying customers. If a page on your site has no use, it should not be there. All your pages should be up-selling your services or products.

Collaboration can be a great thing. Working with other companies or individuals that complement your own. Find businesses that have a similar goal and vision to yourself. Collaborate to a mutually beneficial outcome and produce something that you wouldn't necessarily be able to do on your own. We often have clients that ask for a service that we don't provide ourselves, but we know would benefit them and so we have collaborated with other businesses who we could recommend to our clients.

We are now setting up a website where we are all under one roof to offer clients the whole package from branding, website, SEO/online marketing (which we at Clockwork Moggy offer,) to fitness coaches, personal branding specialist, business mentor, video marketer, printers, social media experts, accountant, IT support and even someone that provides a place for meetings. When you're talking about lead generation and teaming up with other people, you will become stronger and those other businesses all point back to you as well. This is called Entrepreneurs Umbrella.

Poor brand image can hinder your lead generation. If your brand identity and image looks rushed or thrown together or it doesn't give the right impression of what you do, this will lead to confusion and mistrust. Your brand image takes a lot of work to build a good reputation and needs to be consistent across everything you apply it to from business cards, e-newsletters, printed material to your website and social media. Done correctly, it can do wonders but done badly it could make people think twice about doing business with you. This can be quite daunting if you're a new business. It doesn't cost anything to get advice from professionals.

We practice lead generation as often and as creatively as possible through many means - our website (customer journey and sales funnels), social media (brand awareness), SEO (lead generation and Google ranking), video marketing - giving away free, useful information, radio (brand awareness), speaking (brand awareness), workshops (showing that we are experts in our field and helping other companies to learn), business exhibitions (brand awareness), networking (lead generation), and of course, writing a section of a book. We measure where our leads come from to see what gives us our biggest ROI.

So there's just a few tips! Become a full-blown marketing machine and get those leads generating. Managing all of this can be like juggling, and we learned quickly that you cannot possibly do everything yourself, so start with a marketing plan, work out where your budget will go and make contact with people who can help you and advise you along the way.

*Carrie Stay*

By Entrepreneurs for Entrepreneurs!

Lead generation is about putting your marketing strategy before sales. Business networking is therefore part of your marketing in order to get the sales. By networking you are leveraging your business and personal connections to bring you a regular supply of new business. It is an important part of your business strategy and should be prioritised in your diary.

To some, networking means handing out business cards to everyone within 3 feet of you; to others it just means having a conversation to see how you can help people. At the end of the day, people buy from those they know, like and trust unless it's just something they need immediately and then they buy from a traditional shop or an online shop.

We all have competition and lots of other companies or businesses will be selling exactly the same as you. These days people tend to look on their phone or other mobile device to find what they want and check the prices. They might then come back to you to buy the product or service because they know you and you offer a fantastic service.

Networking is therefore a combination of getting to know people and providing the service which your clients are looking for.

Effectively, networking is about building relationships, getting to know people and finding out how you can help them. To be honest, they are not really interested in you! I know that sounds a bit harsh but it's true. They are there to get business and initially are probably not interested in your product or service.

So how do you get the best out of your networking? I always go to a networking event with the intention of making friends, finding out what other people do and seeing how I can help them. At a recent networking event there were 30 people attending, and 7 of them were business coaches of one sort or another. Three more were accountants. Do you think everyone in the room needed any of my services that day? Probably not but by talking to everyone and connecting them to people who can help them, they remember you.

I do a lot of networking and therefore know a lot of people. So I am a great connector and people know that.

Effective networking isn't just about what happens on the day. You don't know who people know; who their circle of influence is. I often follow up with a coffee meeting. When you sit down and chat with someone you find out all sorts of things which don't come out in a one minute pitch.

They tell you about their business, sometimes about their family and often about people they know. You then have the perfect opportunity to offer them a solution either with a product or service or maybe a connection.

Sometimes it doesn't go anywhere but they often remember and come back to you at another time when the time is right for them. This takes time but it's definitely worth it. I've built my business from eating breakfast and drinking tea! I also get asked to speak at events when people know a bit more about me, my background and my story.

Again, this doesn't often happen from a one minute pitch but more often from a 10 minute presentation or maybe speaking at a networking event. I've had amazing results from networking online which has resulted in fabulous connections and opportunities.

Effective networking is about consistency. If you try and go to every networking event you see in your area, you won't do any of it properly and people won't remember you.

You are much better to find a format that works for you, find a networking group that works for you and then attend on a regular basis.

If you are a regular networker, think about the people who come and go or who appear for one or two meetings and then disappear again. Would you recommend them? Probably not because we all have competition and there will be someone new on the block who is consistent and whose name is at the forefront of your mind.

I'm sure we've all witnessed those people who rush in, hand out cards and then disappear. Yes they network regularly but do you remember them. It's all about perception and mindset.

Take the time to get to know people and talk to any new people who are at your regular networking events. Build your circle of trusted people who you would happily recommend to others. It takes time but you will benefit hugely in the long run.

You are probably networking a lot more than you realise! Every time you are out and about talking to people, you are effectively networking.

One weekend I was out with a friend and we decided to pop into the local church where they had a coffee morning. We were sitting drinking a cup of tea and enjoying a piece of cake when an elderly gentleman asked if he could sit with us.

We got talking and he asked if we were local. He then proceeded to tell us about the refurbishment of the church which had just been completed.

The next thing on their agenda was the cleaning of a roof on an outbuilding and he was looking for a roofing contractor. My friend happens to be a roofing contractor so the gentleman then introduced us to the vicar and several of the ladies helping with the coffee morning. One of the ladies turned out to have taught my friends cousin many years ago and remembered the family.

We were then taken to have a look at the outbuilding and asked for a quote to complete the required work. That was networking in a very informal way but a cup of tea led to a fantastic contact and a good possibility of some work.

Networking online is no different to face-to-face networking. Take the time to get to know people, have a chat about their business and their problems and then see if you can help them. Sometimes it's not about selling to them but making a connection for them.

I often connect people who I think can help each other. I know it doesn't earn me any money but do you think the parties remember me? Yes of course they do and they often connect me to interesting people as a result.

One example is someone I've been talking to on LinkedIn. He has a marketing business with online courses and I showed an interest in what he's doing and how he runs his courses. As a result he sent me the videos so that I could see for myself and asked me for my feedback. A few days later he called me and we had a good chat and told each other about our backgrounds and our current businesses.

He then went on to connect me to someone who has a business TV channel. He in turn has been chatting and wants to meet up for a brew to see how we can help each other.

To me, that is a much better way to connect with people and build that relationship. It takes longer but the results are so much better. In this particular example, I now have two really good connections who are interested in collaborating to grow all our businesses.

We all have good connections and can really promote each other to our respective lists which can only be a good thing. It means that our circle of influence has now grown considerably with a few conversations and an abundant mindset that, to share our resources and work together is of benefit to all of us.

So look at your online connections. How often do you chat to them and see how you can help them? Sometimes it can be something as simple as saying *"congratulations"* or *"happy birthday."*

This happened with one of my connections. We'd met a few years ago at a BNI meeting and at that time didn't have much in common so didn't really keep in touch. However, it was Ryan's birthday and it came up on my LinkedIn feed. So I sent the templated email wishing him a happy birthday and asking how he was doing.

We then continued the conversation and realised that his mother lives near me. He was having lunch with her a few days later so we arranged to meet for coffee beforehand. We then discovered that both our businesses had changed considerably. In fact mine is now completely different and when I told him what I was doing he offered to help me with some design issues I was experiencing.

I am also able to help him by promoting his business to my connections and in fact we now have a joint venture which is of benefit to both of us. All this came from a happy birthday!

The key to all of this is engagement. It's no good just connecting to people; you need to engage with them, talk to them and find out how you can help each other. People often ask how to network online. For me it's no different to face-to-face networking. The only difference is that I type rather than speak but it often leads to a phone call or a coffee meeting or sometimes a Skype call.

***Sally Marshall.***

By Entrepreneurs for Entrepreneurs!

# 6 *E*NGAGE

*Most people don't like selling! If you asked them what they thought of car salesmen, double glazing salesmen, insurance salesmen, estate agents or say timeshare salesmen, the answer would probably be an expletive! The problem is we have been conditioned to think selling is a dirty word so when we have to do it ourselves there is a disconnect between our actions and our brains. Incongruence! Selling is just a conversation and most people can talk so it should be quite easy.*

*Yes it is a conversation, and more importantly it is a structured conversation that measures the results you are getting (cause and effect). If you're not getting the sale, adjust your conversation and start asking better questions within your conversation. I see so many salesmen/women telling everyone about their product or service. They should be asking not telling. The rule is "If you're telling, you're not selling!"* **Ash**

A key problem that business owners face with selling seems to stem from the negative perception they, and most people, have towards sales and "salesmen". Additional to that negative bias is the fact that many people don't seem to invest time and genuine interest in developing relationships with people before trying to sell to them. They forget to build rapport and have conversations.

Of course, it's obvious that the overriding challenge, and necessity in business, is to get more sales and higher net worth. After all we're in business to count the money at the end of the day or we'd simply take a 9-5 job. All businesses need remuneration for their services/products, in order to succeed. So with sales being a fundamental, basic foundation for success, isn't it incredible that many business owners are failing in how to sell effectively!

The shortcomings in the sales process arise from a lack of understanding. If most business owners knew that nearly everyone has a negative bias to salesmen and selling, they'd already have an advantage over most of their competitors.

Grasping this basic concept would encourage them towards the best way to create sales. It would forever put a nail in the coffin of traditional pressure sales and concentrate on conversational sales. How to sell is as important a question as who to sell to, where to sell, and what to sell!

It seems to me that the problems stem from; an ignorance about basic human psychology, skill deficits in sales techniques and, a lack of real structure and planning in the sales process. Above all, knowing that selling should be a happy outcome of a natural, balanced conversation. A conversation you should have thought about and have a vision on the ultimate outcome, but one that doesn't ram your business down their throats.

Everyone should learn about effective engagement with others, listening skills and building trust and rapport better to make significant advances in their sales process. It's not just about who you know, but how well you know them and that applies to creating sales relationships as much as any other kind of relationship.

It sounds a bit bonkers (and indeed it has been) but with my business we simply didn't actively "sell" enough. So busy caught up in "doing the doing" and relying on our reputation spreading by word of mouth and networking, that we didn't actually push our business as much as we could. Clients came to us by and large.

With hindsight, for my part, I think that sometimes it was a fear of pushing forward and getting it wrong! I'm sure some of you might relate to this.

The lack of a structured, well-conceived sales process made me feel vulnerable about what and how I was selling the business and our services. I prefer to operate within a background structure that offers focus, but we'd never made time to put it in place. Also if I'd understood the "science" behind selling, the psychology of people a bit better, I would have been much better equipped to build better relationships to win sales and engage with people more confidently.

Don't think I want to act like a sales robot or anything, because then you just come across as insincere and a "hunter". Understanding how "stuff" works does help though.

If I'd learned about the E.N.G.A.G.E sales process (that I've recently learned through the Millionaire Mindset course), then we would have developed a better sales process earlier on.

I also recognise in myself a tendency to adopt a "scarcity" mindset which can make me "want the sale" a bit too keenly! I should just focus on the prospect and think in terms of the prospect. Focusing on their "wants", and actively listening, rather than thinking about my business. I also fell into the trap of negative language patterns in my own head, which created a psychological barrier.

I've learned from the MMS and the Entrepreneurs Business Club I attend every month now, that not only are my own language patterns important but the language patterns of others.

They offer signals to tune into so you can have a better conversation in terms of potential sales outcomes.

I guess, like everything, it all comes down to having a system and process- giving what we do for sales effectiveness in our business, the practice and planning it deserves.

Four areas you could look at, (and which I explored after completing the Millionaires Mindset course), that can help with the "sales process" are;-

**1)** Ditch old habits in your business around selling.

**2)** Embrace an integrity sales process built around the E.N.G.A.G.E model, a 6 step process that builds on conversational, integrity selling rather than pressure selling.

**3)** Adopt the P.A.C.T philosophy of doing business and engaging with people, and follow the know, like and trust model.

**4)** Learn about structuring language and conversations intentionally and with forethought. Just like other important stuff, you should plan your conversations – not the exact wording you're going to use, but just the outcome you'd like to get from a sales-related conversation.

Pre-thinking a conversation doesn't mean you need to be prescriptive in delivering it, because that is NOT what you want to do. Once you've thought about what sort of conversations you want to have, you can relax and enjoy them.

By Entrepreneurs for Entrepreneurs!

HABITS- **H**abits **A**re **B**attles **I**n **T**hought **S**tructures (H.A.B.I.T.S)- What I mean with my own slightly dodgy acronym is that old habits battle against new concepts in our heads and unless we practice the new concepts repeatedly and with vigour, the bad habits will prevail. It's a battlefield, and often, new ideas are slain by the army of old habits we have!

INTEGRITY SALES -In sales, the traditional four step sales process of opening (qualifying), gathering information, presenting your proposal, and finally closing the deal is a habit. If, however, we move to a better system, one based on a six step integrity sales process such as E.N.G.A.G.E, we can have a conversation, that, behind the scenes, has some structure to it.

We can sell with confidence, or more importantly we can offer reasons for customers to buy. We get so wrapped up in our own business concerns that we forget to talk in the way our prospects want. It's the only real way to influence people – as Lloyd George, Prime Minister during the First World War stated *"You have to bait the hook to suit the fish"*.

P.A.C.T-People buy from people they know, and like and trust when presented with choice, and as most of us have competitors, there is plenty of choice out there. You'd have to have a particularly niche offering to be the only option, and that would probably change pretty quickly once other people realised what a goldmine you were sitting on!

So learning the best way to be known and remembered, the quickest route to be liked, and the key to trust is going to serve us all better for sales as well as generally. Ash Lawrence talks about P.A.C.T which stands for Promises, Activate ears, Compassion and Trust. I think this anagram is a great rule of thumb for conduct in sales as well as in your wider business.

In a nutshell;

Keep your **P**romises – if you say you'll do something then just do it!

**A**ctivate your ears - listen to people properly – not to just prepare a response but to truly understand them even if you don't agree with them. Listening well shows respect and makes you stand out because most people don't listen properly.

Have **C**ompassion – don't think in terms of right or wrong, your side versus their side, but think of a better way. If you haven't already read or listened to "The 3rd Alternative" by Stephen Covey then I urge you to. A true door stop at 56 chapters, but it's brilliant and you can do chunks at a time. I listen to it in my car to and from work. I get some odd looks in traffic queues sometimes, when the window's down so, Alfie, my much loved Border Terrier/Cairn Terrier cross, can stick his head out, but who cares!

**T**ruth – obvious yes, but may people don't hold this as a pillar of their business! Be truthful with others and equally importantly, be truthful with yourself.

These four pillars alone will give you stand out- something discussed in this book as well. Remember that personal/individual stand out will help you sell out!

Every entrepreneur knows that it never stops in business– it's continually evolving and so it should. Change happens everywhere, all the time.

By Entrepreneurs for Entrepreneurs!

We all need to embrace change and make changes in our businesses. That way, we can journey from how we do it now, to a better way, and ultimately the best way.

One of the first things I've done to help me effect change in my business as far as selling is concerned, is revisit a specific book that stands the test of time – "How to Win Friends and Influence People" by Dale Carnegie. Written back in 1936 it's still as relevant and powerful in helping me become a better communicator and relationship builder.

If you've never read it, read it, and if you've already read it, then read it again (now there's a tongue twister). Whenever I'm faced with any challenge I try to find someone whose already worked it out and take their "shortcut". So books have become a vital resource for that, and the Millionaires Mindset course encourages lots of reading, which has got me back into this healthy habit!

*"Not all readers are leaders, but all leaders are readers"* (Harry Truman, 33rd President of the USA (1945-1953)

We are focusing on the conversation of selling and not imposing our "wants" on prospects but instead, preparing the prospect to want to buy from us and thereby making the prospect feel more in control of the buying experience.

We're aiming to give the best consistent experience regardless of the staff member delivering that to the prospect. We're also working on various product tiers and service levels to cover different budgets, and build more sales avenues that fit customer's requirements. So, for example with one of our best- sellers, the polo shirt, we would quote for a budget, mid-level and premium polo on most quotations.

Or with our service levels on promotional items- express service, standard service, and DIY service (our online drop ship ordering portal).

Something else that boosts the sales process is social proof, so we are actively seeking more testimonials and referrals from our clients. Of course any IP content you can build and broadcast will help drive the sales to your door – it's back to the "know" and "trust" bit.

I've learnt to understand and predict our prospects/customer fears and objections so I can overcome them in advance! For example, sizing is always a concern with ordering garments, and creates a barrier to purchase, so we offer size sets for clients to take back to their workforce for accurate sizing. Other people are concerned about how their logo will translate in embroidery or textile print so we provide physical samples.

We've identified specific sales targets on our new office whiteboard, and discuss the type of conversation content we'd like to have with them, and whose the "best fit" to have that conversation. We have leveraging at the forefront of our minds as well, so we can leverage sales from existing contacts and in order to make this successful we have to think about what we can do for them first to build the "reciprocal love"!

Our business has been trading for over 15 years now, and as a limited company since 2000. Yet, up until recently we haven't concentrated enough on a consistently targeted sales process to significantly move us onwards. Too busy being busy!

However now that our focus is on driving our business to the next level, and we've restructured the roles and responsibilities within our business, to define the sales role and sales accountability better, (having taken advice from Ash), we are making significant inroads. Wherever we "sell" we remember it requires a natural, genuine, respectful conversational approach.

The results speak for themselves. In terms of financials, we have exceeded our sales targets consistently since the Millionaires Mindset course, and recently reset our monthly target by doubling it ten days into that month, because we'd exceeded it already. We've also reached last year's turnover level in eight months of this year, and improved our profit margin, and there's still four months to go until our financial year end!

"What gets measured gets changed" is our new mantra, along with "Find it, Focus on it, Finish it". Both "*Ashisms*" (ie from Ash Lawrence).

We realise we've been committing a "crime" in our business for too long now - not using the skills we have to push our business forward. Maybe you can relate to this too. As a crime it was coming with a hefty sentence- one of frustration and missed opportunities. We were doing time in our business but not achieving our potential, but it's changing now!

Don't "do time" in your business – make it a liberating journey to sales success!

***Rachel Cowell***

Sales is always an interesting subject when you speak to other business owners. There are many different takes on how this should be done from the softly softly approach all the way through to the straight up manipulation!

Having spent the last 8 years as a PT, I can safely say I've had plenty of practice and tried pretty much every technique. The most interesting thing was that the harder I tried, the worse I got. It's important we understand the difference between Ten out of 10 (lead generation) and Engage (sales). What we are talking about is the process of converting leads which, ultimately, comes down to a conversation between two humans.

The biggest problem I find businesses struggling with when I'm looking to buy a product or service is that it all comes across so forced, over rehearsed and unnatural. Everyone you know can give you lots of stories about a sleazy salesman trying to manipulate them into buying something. The problem with a manipulation is people know they are being manipulated!

This doesn't have to mean a structured, perfectly executed and objection shattering speech. It can also be a painfully awkward conversation at the end of a training session where the personal trainer stutters and mumbles out a barely audible *"can you pay me please?"* Both of which leave the client feeling uncomfortable and like they want to get as far away as they can …….. not great for making a sale.

My first experience of networking was a perfect example of how NOT to do it. I had bought some business cards, pumped myself full of caffeine and headed off to a local networking group with 40 other business owners. I spent the first half an hour bouncing around the room telling people about myself without asking any questions, while I simultaneously rammed my business card down their throats. My one minute was some super technical and un-engaging spiel about the dangers of eating bread and then I left really quickly because I had to go back to work for a client. I remember getting back to the studio, counting my business cards, realising I had given out 20 and thinking "I'll just wait by the phone for my 20 calls to come through". What a complete twat! Obviously I didn't get any phone calls.

I've been networking at least 4 times a month for the last 4 years now and even run my own group. You'll be pleased to know that I've drastically changed my strategy of being a complete twat to a much more successful relationship building style. I can honestly say that I have successfully built two businesses almost exclusively from going to networking meetings.

There is nothing more powerful then a solid referral from a friend when it comes to converting a stranger into a new client. My good friend and mentor Ash, (who also happens to own the networking company I work with), told me very early on the 'golden rule of business' ….. are you ready?

*"People buy from people that they know, like and trust".*

What this means is that business is built on trust, and trust is a process. First you have to know someone, if you never meet new people then you can't get to know them. Once you know them, if you don't treat them with care and respect they will never like you. People who don't like you will never trust or do business with you! Alternatively, you constantly meet new people, you treat them with respect, build meaningful relationships and you will become friends. Those people will like you, buy from you and even work with you.

Over time you will build trust and then those new friends will become one of THE BEST referral sources for your business. Beautiful!

I absolutely love this! The reason I chose to write this chapter in the book you're reading right now is because the, golden rule of business is based purely on the relationships you have with other people. Every business in the world would go bankrupt if there were no people to buy their product or service, and the key to being great at sales comes down purely to your ability to build meaningful relationships. That's why this is the most important chapter in this book.

The conversations you have with potential new clients is where the rubber hits the road for your business. If you do this in a manipulative, selfish or nervous way …… your business will fail, FACT.

The great thing is, this means anyone can be great at sales without any training or years of experience. All you need to be able to do is connect with people on a deeper level, be genuinely interested and put their needs first.

It's time to forget your ABC's…

Anyone who has had any sales training of any kind would have heard the acronym '**A**lways **B**e **C**losing'. What this means is if you're a salesman in a meeting with a potential client, you should always aim to close the deal by the time the meeting finishes. This could even be a telephone call or a salesman holding a clipboard in a high street stopping you as you walk past. The goal with this is to maximise their time as a salesman by locking in the sale.

The outcome for you, as the consumer, is that it gets right on your tits! At best you will have your time wasted, at worst you will be forced into buying something that you don't really want and instantly suffer from buyers remorse (more on this later). For me this whole concept is completely backwards.

If you are constantly trying to 'close' people you are shutting down the conversation by trying to end it. What if that person doesn't want what you are selling? Not only are you not listening to what they are saying, but you're actually destroying the potential for them liking you ..... not good! Furthermore, what if they don't want your product right now but may do in the future? After trying to close them and making them dislike you, they're going to use someone else who can provide the same thing as you and hasn't made them feel uncomfortable.

Now, imagine if the goal in any potential sales situation was to always leave it 'open'. What I mean by this is you simply having a conversation with someone where you really listen to what their challenge is, you offer your solution and if its not the right fit, you say "well thank you for taking the time to come and see me.

If your situation changes I'm always here and if there's anything else I can do to help then please do not hesitate to ask." What do you think that person is going to feel like leaving that conversation? The exact opposite to what being 'closed' feels like.

By always leaving conversations 'open' you have left a perfect opportunity for them to come back, treated them with respect and formed the basis for a relationship. If they are ready for your product at a later date will they come back to you?

Of course they will! Even more than that, you can guarantee that if one of their friends needs what you sell they will refer them straight to you.

A much better acronym would be '**A**lways **B**e **C**onversing'. Why not focus on simply having an open conversation where your only focus is on building that relationship? You'll be amazed at how much this will positively affect your business.

Stop manipulating, start communicating! The problem with trying to manipulate people is that they know they are being manipulated! There are so many different types of sales tactics, structures and methods. They're all based around closing and they're all a form of manipulation. There was a insurance salesman tactic used that perfectly highlights my point and it goes like this;

Greets - The salesman meets the couple at their house, introduces himself and is invited inside.

Relaxes - Builds rapport with couple, asks them about their family, hobbies and holidays. Compliments them on a beautiful house, accepts a cup of tea and sits down in the front room to chat.

Disturbs - Asks the husband to show him something outside. When outside points at his wife sitting alone in the front room through the window and says "look at your wife sitting there on her own, now imagine you are gone and your wife is left alone just like that. You wouldn't want her to have to worry now would you?"

Relaxes - Takes back inside and explains about all the benefits of the life insurance cover plan including how his wife will be looked after in the case of his death and vice versa.

Closes - Gets the deal signed up with a nice little commission.

This is an extreme case but it shows how standard sales training will use some kind of structure to overcome objections, provide the solution and then close. When you manipulate people in this way they suffer from buyer's remorse. This is the feeling you get when you've bought something that you don't need and you feel crap because of it. This is bad because people who aren't happy tell other people how they feel. If a reputation can takes years to make, and just one stupid mistake to ruin, then these conversations can be deadly for your business.

Another poorly used strategy is 'rapport building'. Don't get me wrong, building rapport is how you turn strangers into friends. The problem occurs when you meet someone who is fresh from a 'rapport building' workshop. Just like a cowboy with a loaded gun they are poised and ready to deliver a torrent of techniques! Everything from mirroring, reading eye movements, repeating the person's name, paraphrasing the other persons answer, leaning in, leaning back and the list goes on and on ……

People who are focused on all these things are missing the one most important part of a conversation, listening! We have two ears and one mouth for a reason. By the time you finished mirroring their body position and reading their eye patterns you've completely missed what they said. Having watched 100's of consultations take place I can promise you that there is nothing more uncomfortable than a person who won't stop repeating a persons name or nodding along incessantly. Just like any other form of manipulation, it makes the client feel really awkward and guaranteed to not want to be in that situation again, no sale.

The crazy thing is that the less you try, the better you get! That cowboy with the loaded gun was me, I did it for years desperately trying to put everything into practice all in a 30 min consultation and you know what, it was shit.

The moment I stopped all the techniques and genuinely listened, simply having a friendly and open conversation, my conversion rate went up to 100%. When you relax and really listen to what the person is saying you will do ALL OF THE THINGS listed above automatically. You can't help it. The human brain can detect a facial expression change in a nano second, body language and tone of speech are how we've communicated with each other for 1000's of years.

You don't need to spend your time consciously trying to do it. The number one way, without fail, to get better at building rapport -have more meaningful conversations.

For more in depth information of how to build truly awesome relationships check out 'The Go-Giver" and 'The Go-Giver Sells More' by Bob Burg.

*"Some people bring happiness wherever they go, some whenever they go."*

Ultimately to be good at sales you just need to be yourself. If you have an awesome product or service and someone wants what you have, the actual sales conversation is easy.

When its forced, its unnatural and nobody wins. I can promise you that if your main focus is building a meaningful relationship with that person then they will become a personal sales person for you whether they want your product or not.

Either way by making sure you leave them feeling understood and respected you'll be spreading a bit of happiness. Don't be the person that only creates happiness when they've left the room.

***Ross Cowan.***

Being in business is about making money, this is a fact! Any business no matter what the service provided needs to make money to be a business. I love what I do, but loving the service I offer will not bring money into the business without a strategy, a sales strategy. .

Most business owners try too hard, push too hard. People, clients know when they are being sold to; the hard sale just doesn't work. I know this because I hate it being done to me.

I've been to many beauty spa/salons and experienced facial treatments that have been the most unrelaxing ever, leaving me with the conclusion that I would never go back. Throughout the so called pamper session/facial, the therapist didn't shut up. Every product she put on my face from revitalizing cleanser to the rich firming moisturizer was explained in depth, then at the end of my "beautiful tranquil" (irritating) facial, I was given my very own prescription of products that I should buy...... OK! That sucks!

I never wanted to be that type of salon that would make people run the other way. I was so anti sales that I never did it. I never really tried to sell anything for fear that I would scare people off. All because of my own experience (a somewhat bad one).

I've lost clients because I was too nervous to say anything in fear of putting people off. Oh dear how silly I sound, but that's what tends to happen in most businesses. Clients are not asked to re-book, or a product is not suggested in case of scaring them off.

I've worked in many set ups from a small room in hairdressers, to running a large spa in a health centre and now have my own beauty salon.

I've been employed, self-employed working alone, and also employed people to create a great team. All situations have been such a learning curve. I spent more money than I made (with no regrets, just very valuable lessons learned).

The salon I have at present is perfect for the self-employed, offering a fantastic base for different therapists to work as part of a team and have all the benefits of running their own business with the support of like-minded people.

I have learnt the hard way with sales and lost so many client opportunities, but what I know today is people will buy what they need. When someone wants and needs the service I'm offering it's easier to sell. It's even easier because I believe and love the service I offer. I speak with passion, appreciation and confidence about the subject.

Whilst trying to market my business and get more clients, I discovered networking through a good friend and met Ash Lawrence the owner and founder of ABC networking. This is where I was introduced to the Millionaire Mindset course. This is a business course delivered over a one year time scale.

I had been in business a long time before, but kept making the same mistakes. I wore all the hats; all the admin, the marketing, training staff etc. The list goes on. So the course came along at the right time for me I was so chuffed to be in a position to be shown how to run my business and be successful.

I was eager to learn and had the willingness to listen and make the suggested changes. All be it somewhat difficult changes but all made an amazing difference to my business. As part of the one year course, I was taught about the 6 'STEP SALES PROCESS'; this was so eye opening and has changed my approach completely. So what is the '6 STEP SALES PROCESS' I hear you ask?

Being part of the mindset course I learned this process in detail as well as a sales strategy, (the one I talked about earlier). Having a sales strategy is paramount. The funny thing is, it's built in me now, and I just presume everyone knows about it, until I witness someone not doing it, and it reminds me how I used to be. However I'm not perfect with the process, so I'm constantly learning and revisiting parts of the 6 'STEP SALES PROCESS'. It was pointed out that the first three steps of the '6 Step Sales Process' are the most important, because this is where you'll overcome the objections of the sale. I'm going to talk about step two.

Step two is 'POSITIONING', so what is positioning? It's about being the 'go to' person in my particular field, so now I needed to work out how? Positioning is about 'owning' a space in someone's mind. For example, if I say to you, "you need to buy a vacuum cleaner", you would automatically think about 'Hoover'. 'Hoover' is a brand name that's already in your mind.

So for me, what I now needed to do, was to work out how I would be able to own the space in someone's mind? By that I mean, when someone needs hair removal the first thing that pops into their mind is Deborah Jones, Positive Pathways (ME!)

I previously said I love what I do, I believe what I do and I always get great results. So how do I get this information over to my prospective new clients without ramming it down their throats? And to become the first person that pops into anyone's mind when looking for hair removal.

It starts with my WHY? Why do I do what I do? Well of course there is the income, the money I get from the service is important to continue to run the business, but it's more than the money. People who know and trust me already can see it's more than money.

It's so clear, everything I say and do relating to the service I offer. The passion, the love I portray! The fact that I get excited with my clients is real. I get excited when a client becomes over-whelmed with joy at the results. That's my WHY! Because I care! The privilege I feel when sharing someone's happiness, watching the joy in their face, knowing their escape from despair has arrived!

My WHY = RESULTS- I care. I really honestly care, being compassionate and personal to get the results to make someone feel great, to change life's and raise self-esteem. With this in mind, how do I sell my service? I have many videos and written testimonials that state previous client experiences. All the recommendations from my clients are my influencers, talking about their own experience. What it was like, what I did for them and how they feel now.

Telling their personal stories, with pictures showing what it was like before their treatment, during their treatment and what it is like now. All this information is to help another person get identification, clarifying through the story, why they would choose my service over the other salon down the road that offers the same. Why they would trust my service over someone else.

I've learnt it's about building trust. When a new prospect can see and hear about results, trusted accounts time and time again, saying the same things, having the same message, they in turn start to trust the process.

I never need to change the message because it's a clear message and its fact! I've created video's to educate, and putting my face to a name on my website has helped stamp my intent to be the go to person, and it works. Oh my, it really works. Being brave enough to stick my neck on the line, to stand in front of my fellow peers and project confidence and compassion. Also having many clients as my pioneers speaking about me, telling others about their positive experience has been so amazing!

For me today my business is doing well. I have an outstanding service with a premium price, and a profound confidence to work with people who know and trust my process. I'm truly grateful to be in a position where I learnt how to do business, this has reinforced my success level. The experience I've had with business growth over the last 4 years, being in the right place at the right time, to discover there are others ways to run a business and get success without feeling overwhelmed.

The day to day tasks in business seemed so dull, and a lack of enthusiasm that caused me to feel demotivated. I even felt at times maybe I needed to look to do something else, or to add a service or change my service to make me feel more enthused. I didn't need something else. What I know now is that I needed to be part of a group that helps me to overcome all of this, not to run away. I needed help to keep learning and developing both personally and in business, so after finishing the Millionaire Mindset course I went on to be part of an accountability group, called the Entrepreneurs Business Club. Fabulous! Being willing to learn, being held accountable and really moving forward to achieve goals!

*__Deborah Jones.__*

# 7 *ME*THOD

*Michael Gerber wrote in his bestselling business book "The E-Myth Revisited" systems and processes run businesses, people run systems and processes!" From making the tea to being the Chief Executive Officer in any business it all needs systems and processes. One of the biggest things that holds businesses back is the reluctance to put efficient systems and processes into their businesses!*

*It really isn't rocket science people... The goal of every business should be to move from good, to better, to best and then document every part of that process. If you are one of the myriad of business owners saying you don't have enough hours in the day, I would suggest to you that you have very poor systems and processes in your business!*
**Ash**

Most business owners switch off if you mention systems and processes but they are a key part of any business, particularly if you want to grow and start employing staff. Without systems and processes it becomes increasingly difficult to take a break from your business, let alone a holiday. If you have a day off sick, then it's quite possible the business will stop for that day and therefore the income will as well. That isn't a position which is sustainable for very long for any business.

So what are systems and processes? You probably already have processes by which you run your business but I would hazard a guess that most of them are in your head! Documenting all your processes sounds very time consuming and it is to start with, but if you take it one step at a time and start to write down everything you do into a word document, then you can add to it as you go along.

To put it into context, think about McDonalds. They started as a small business in exactly the same way as the rest of us but have built a global business based on systems and processes. If you go anywhere in the world, the burgers are exactly the same. That doesn't happen by accident! They have documented absolutely everything they do in their business from how they place the pickles on the burgers to how long the French fries are in the fryer. They then have a document which they can use to train staff in every outlet.

As businesses grow and more staff are employed, a training program, based on the systems and processes in the business, is essential.

Even for a small business, having a resource for staff which they can dip into themselves as and when they need it, makes your life so much easier. Business owners who interfere in the every-day operations are a nightmare both for the business and for the people who work in it!

Having processes in place means that you can step away from the business and leave other people to get on with what needs to be done. In reality, they will probably do it better and quicker than you can.

So where do you start?

Look at all the processes in your business. The easiest ones to start with are probably the bookkeeping and maybe social media. For most business owners, the accounts are their worst area and so it is an easy thing to delegate.

However, you still need to have a process in place so that the bookkeeper has all the information they need in a timely manner and is therefore able to perform the job efficiently.

Identify the steps in the process and document each one.

Some examples are:

- Invoicing of clients – how will they get the sales data?

- Receipt and payment of invoices for goods/services you've purchased.

- You might only want a bookkeeper for a few hours a week or a month so document how and when they will work.

- What passwords they will need?

- Do they need access to any folders or files?

- Set up a system for coding particular expense types so that you can run reports.

- A regular review of the accounts so that you can see how the business is performing.

All of the above needs to be documented in details so that someone else can follow it and carry out the actions required. It is a good idea to get someone to test the process who doesn't know anything about the business.

We all do things automatically and when you get a complete novice to try it, you will probably find one or two things which you have missed!

Systems and processes are something which are always evolving. Once you have all the basics in place for every process in your business, you will be able to look at ways to improve them until you get to best practice.

Have a look at what others in your sector do and how they do it. Do they automate processes that you are currently doing manually? Technology is changing so fast that it's a good idea to keep up-to-date with what's available. Automating a process frees up time to focus on something else which perhaps needs a bit more attention.

Everyone complains that there aren't enough hours in the day but by putting in place processes which other people can follow and automating as much as possible, you will be amazed at how much time you are able to free up. Either to focus on the areas you really want to work on or maybe to reduce your hours on a regular basis.

Businesses often run better without the boss! Getting the right people and the right processes in place gets rid of the boss from the day-to-day operations of a business.

If you're not yet convinced, have a look at your own business or that of someone you know. See how much time you spend answering the same question over and over or carrying out a task which you don't particularly like or don't really want to do.

If someone else can do the task at a lower cost than your own hourly rate, then you need to put a process in place and start to delegate. You will be amazed at the difference it makes.

To see how this works in action, watch an episode of "Ramsay's Kitchen Nightmares" or the "Hotel Inspector". You will soon see that in each failing business there is the same issue. Very often the business owner is very controlling, doesn't trust anyone to do anything, doesn't know what is going on in the business and doesn't have any processes in place.

Quite often the staff don't have proper job descriptions, don't have any idea what is going on and are really demotivated. In every case, the solution is to review what is actually happening in the business, see where the problems are and focus on systems and processes to get everything back on track.

The business owner themselves often resist the changes but once they are in place, they see the difference in the takings, the staff and their happy customers. Happy customers mean more business which in turns means bigger profits and motivated staff.

Once you have your processes in place, you will need to review them on a regular basis just to make sure that you are getting the results that you expect. If something isn't working properly, go back to the processes and see how it can be changed to improve it and therefore improve the results.

A great example of this is the MP expenses in the House of Commons a few years ago. There was a process in place but as everyone found out, in a very public way, the process wasn't working. When the process was looked at in detail, it was discovered that it was based on trust to a large extent and had not been audited for a considerable time.

The process itself was therefore changed so that MP's expenses were looked at in a more holistic way so that any anomalies were picked up immediately. The indicators were there to show that there was a problem but no-one looked in detail until it was published day after day in a national newspaper.

Although it is unlikely that your business would be held up to scrutiny in such a public way, you don't want to find yourself in such a situation, where the rules are being used in a way which isn't beneficial to your business.

Unfortunately however good your process is, there is always someone who will find a shortcut without really understanding the consequences.

A business which had a very rigorous process for authorising invoices suddenly found that several invoices had been paid twice. In theory this couldn't happen but it had. When the process was looked at in detail it was discovered that the automated part was fine; the problem came with the parts of the process which involved human intervention.

To save time, someone had found a work around which had tricked the system into thinking the invoices were different and therefore able to be paid. It was a costly lesson but the process was then changed so that it couldn't happen again in the future.

To sum up, systems and processes are a vital part of a successful business which is often overlooked. Getting to grips with documenting them and creating an operating manual for your business will save you a lot of time in the long run and will make your business much more efficient and profitable. It will also add to the value of your business should you decide to sell it at some time in the future.

*Sally Marshall*

Coming from a background of teaching, having a wage each month, having a good pension, was one thing but I was always moaning about my work load. Maybe at the time the only plus I could ever see was, I was employed with a secure job, (I now understand nothing is secure in life, especially paid employment). However I had a vision of a little treatment room with burning scented candles, dim lights, offering beauty treatments, making people happy, working for myself, no boss. Just me! That's how I saw it in my head.

How wonderful each day would be! I often thought about what I could earn per hour, and time off when I wanted it. I thought about the cost's, such as the room rental, treatment insurance, products I would need etc. That's about all I thought about, I didn't think much past that. Silly me!

Starting my business was an exciting venture! I had this vision; offering beauty treatments in a little room, decorated in pastel shades (decorating costs), making people happy (customer service), working for myself (no secure income), hey but no boss! Yay! Just me! That's how I saw it in my head. How wonderful it would be.

The reality was very different, but I didn't see any of this until I was in it and boy it was hard and frustrating. Oh my goodness, I found it so very difficult trying to work with my clients, the very thing I'd dreamed about. . The hard faced reality was: accounts, marketing, council licensing, clinical waste, websites, networking – phew and the rest! I felt alone and washed out, but I wasn't going to give up. What I did next was even crazier. I just threw more money at the business! Then more money, and yet more money, and remortgaged the house for a substantial amount too!

The unmanageability with the finance was vast. It was putting pressure on my relationships, also my suppliers and all this kept me in constant fear. I was providing the services to clients, the marketing, creating my own leaflets then doing leaflet drops with my husband, writing my own website, doing the accounts, cleaning the salon, running a family, a home, dealing with growing teenage boys with teenage problems. I was run ragged! What happened to the time off when I wanted and paid leave – oh dear!

Being in business for a number of years now has made me so aware of how incredibly difficult I made it for myself. Looking back now makes me cringe (just a bit), but hey I've learnt so much over the years. I knew no difference. But now I do know and I'm so very grateful for the journey I've had, and importantly I would love to prevent anyone else from making the same mistakes.

I find myself observing new businesses and really want to help, but sometimes the new business owner just doesn't want to listen. That was me! I knew how, I knew exactly what needed to be done, when to do it, and I needed to do it, myself!

It was all about TRUST...... I just couldn't trust anyone to do it how I did it. You see, "it's my business, my baby, my reputation etc. etc...."

It has taken many years of mistakes (lessons) and lots of money to discover I just cannot do this on my own. Now that to me was a massive discovery. I was introduced to networking a number of years ago and that's where I started to see I needed people to help me to move forward in my business. Not necessarily clients, but people who had experience of running a business.

This was the key to help me know what clients I needed? How would I find the right clients? How would they find me? How would I look after the clients when I had them? How would I communicate with the clients? How I could successfully operate my business and more!!!!!!

Even when I found out all the answers to the above, I still needed help, a system to operate from. This became more apparent when I employed my first staff member. I spent hours and hours of my time teaching her what I did, showing her how and the why of the business. Lots and lots of time which equals money!

Whilst I was still plodding along sharing my business knowledge verbally, I continued networking and met all types of people with different businesses. I became aware I needed to avoid some people who were merely out for their own gain (my money) and had no intention of building relationships. I realise now that networking is all about building relationships, a community of friends. I now have a vast number of contacts (friends). People who help me, and I them!

Networking also gave me access to a business course with Ash Lawrence; called the 'Millionaire Mindset'(MMS), a 12 month course teaching the 12 steps to running a successful business, which I've mentioned already. This was when the change really happened for me and my business. I learnt how to run my business.

The group had a mix of different business owners, all who were struggling with their business for one reason or another. It was the best thing I've ever been involved with. Each month we were given reading to complete and coursework. It was so enlightening and sometimes an emotional challenge.

I learnt that when anyone decides to become a business owner, there are important factors that have to be addressed for the business to be a success and to have long term growth; 1) a clear business strategy (I learnt this on the course) and 2) a clear personal belief system (personal development also is learnt on the course). Having both qualities helped me, increased my courage to keep moving forward.

I learnt so much, but that doesn't mean I now do it all perfectly. I do not, but I have moved forward more in the last five years to a point that I can see the growth. I still need to revisit things I've previously learnt to keep on track, but I'm pretty sure that's normal with everything in life.

One of the areas I learnt was about systems and processes. I had been teaching my staff member the how and the why etc. verbally, but was shown the importance of writing it down. Creating a manual is gold dust, especially when she did leave. I had clear information showing how things were done for a new staff member to use.

On the course, we covered the business growth model. In the advanced growth stage, there are 6 characteristics of business - the third being functionality. When the business is functioning in tip top order with clear, precise systems then people can work through the process effectively.

Demonstrating how easy it is to follow instructions to operate in the salon from day to day without me being there! I found an amazing discovery! To learn how to have a set of books with instructions (my instructions) has made it so easy to delegate – effective delegation is the most important part for me.

It has shown me how I can move the business I love forward and still have it operate exactly how I originally saw it!

What I've leant through the many years of being a business owner is amazing. The beauty is I can continue to learn and to change. My biggest achievement is to work through fear and accept change, because there will always be change. Change is where I'm at today.

My salon is operated by a manual which is at present is being changed and updated. There are self-employed therapists working in a functioning salon. They all follow the systems that I put in place, how I saw my business and adhere to the process. I am excited about the future and realise there will be some hurdles that will come my way as there have been many that I've climbed.

I know there'll be more change as the salon grows, but I will embrace this and ensure I continue to develop my own knowledge, because unless I change with the change, I'll get stuck and won't be able to move.

After completing my 12 months on the MMS, I just knew I needed to continue in a similar way. Meeting each month, going through areas of my life and also my business to extend the growth. Today I am a member of a business accountability group, Entrepreneurs Business Club (EBC).

This is paramount to my own personal growth and it has been a value tool for business growth. The other business owners that are part of the group also have different business experience to bring to the group. Our ideas and challenges can be extremely complex and we are all supportive, encouraging and importantly business friends.

Ash Lawrence runs our group. He has years of business experience which is a major plus, he guides us with areas that need improvement, giving us time and valuable insight from his own business knowledge which in turn helps us to discover the best route to take to move forward. I am very grateful!

***Deborah Jones***

As a business owner that's used to working for myself I always thought I could do it all on my own. I never needed any systems and processes to make my business work!

At one time in my business, I reviewed some advertising budgets and started networking in a network called ABC networking, where I met a chap called Ash Lawrence. Better known today as the #FlipFlopPyscho.

These network meetings were held at 442 Club in Gillingham. Ash told 10 minute stories giving examples in his or someone else's business – it was great business coaching if you listened well.

Through this networking, I heard about his two hour seminar which introduced the Millionaire Mindset course. So in 2013 I booked onto the seminar to see what it was all about.

After going to this business seminar I learnt that I needed to take action and that "cause and effect" would make a difference. On the two hour seminar I learnt many things; one I remember well was about the five stages of business growth model - hearing that in a business you start off in a excited moment then level up into frantic and when your business is up and running into a place where you're in a comfortable position, you then kind of forget about working in your business and take your eye off things. This is where I really was, when it started to fall apart, you then have to start all over again.

I made a few changes within the first month of going to the Mindset seminar and made extra money which actually paid for the complete Millionaire Mindset course. The full course started in the January so I had a month to wait but it was well worth the wait.

I continued the good changes I had made which did continue to help finance matters.

I soon realised after a few days of the mindset course that I really didn't want to just work for myself but to change this I was going to need my business full of systems and processes so I could get over my major issues of trust.

One of the main problems I identified with very soon was all the systems and processes I used for myself were all in my head. If I asked anyone to help me at a busy time or do anything I had to show them exactly what I needed to do every single time and even then they may not do it how I wanted them to.

Most business owners are running around like nutters just doing lots of things, being busy and not actually earning any money at all. They're working in their business constantly from when they get up to when they go to bed and hardly a penny to show for it.

Most self-employed people don't realise that this is happening until it's probably too late, when their mortgage payment has not gone through or their balance is in the red and then get yet another bill. Soon they are just getting behind continuously. I'm glad to say it never got that bad for me before I started to do something about it.

In my industry there were major changes that started happening. Hardware became more reliable, and it was just the software clients were having trouble with, as well as virus issues causing a lot of new client's problems. I started doing this with remote support and not physically going to them. Most issues could be looked at without moving from my office.

Remote support was the way forward for all our clients. If we did not offer this, we'd fall short of the services our competitors were offering at the time. However, the onsite calls gave me more income with the call out charges and on site fees.

It took around 3 months for me to identify the reason our income had diminished over the last year. We weren't charging for the remote support service correctly. It then became a struggle earning the wages I needed each month to pay my bills and keep a roof over my family's heads. I knew something had to change in my business or I'd need to get a full time employed job.

One thing in business you have to do is make a change to see a different result. So my change was to then send letters and emails to all our clients telling them any remote support we undertook was now to be a chargeable job. After all it was my time they were paying for.

This went down with most of our clients OK. We had the odd one that could not understand why we were going to charge for remote support, as we were not being called out on site. Guess this is the mindset of some client's- you will never win them all.

This started to turn my business back around so I was making enough to get by but it was still attracting less revenue than before with onsite call earning (by the hour). Clients appeared to all have financial issues and were making cut backs, trying to find ways to budget and save money.

Working on my own was contributing to me losing revenue, as I couldn't offer remote support and be onsite at the same time.

On the MMS course, we were learning the SYSTEMS approach – 7 layers or areas in business we all need to get right to make the business run itself. One of the seven steps I really needed in this, "SYSTEM," was "METHOD," better known as "systems and processes". This was about 7 months into the course. I never thought I needed them working on my own, but this was when I realised I didn't want to work just on my own anymore. I needed someone to work in my business while I worked on my business.

I found it extremely hard to let myself trust another to do the personal job I did for all my customers, and thought my customers only wanted to deal with me and only wanted me to fix their issues. In my head if I let another person fix the issues and they did not do it the way I did, and messed up, I would loss the client.

My wife worked with me and I thought I had all the trust in the world with everything she did, but then I found I actually didn't even trust her! OK not in the way you may think of but work trust was a definite issue. Turns out I was a control freak and I was advised to read a book called "Speed of Trust" by Stephen Covey.

As I listened to the audio book I realised that it wasn't about trusting someone to do a job correctly, but about learning to trust them until they showed me they couldn't be trusted.

Listening on, it pointed out little minor things. I recognised that, for example, I wasn't trusting my wife. She would go out to make a cup of tea and a sandwich for lunch and I would find myself "helping" her and almost taking over doing it! In my head I was helping to complete the task. In reality, this was me wanting to take control.

Not trusting her to make the sandwich in the way I liked it; buttered, cutting the tomatoes too thick or making the tea too strong or weak. I'd go to see if she was doing it right. This was the subconscious in me and I hadn't recognised it until reading the book. It made me aware of a lot of trust issues I had.

So I reprogrammed myself to just sit and wait, and when she made a sandwich or a cup of tea, I would just say "OK, yes please, if you want any help please ask" – a simple phrase but a huge lesson practiced.

How did this show in my business? A few times previously, when I took on a work experience student, I would show them how to do a task. Instead of letting them try and get on with it, I would let them start, and as soon as they stopped to asked a question or double check something, I would find myself slowly taking over and doing it myself.

I didn't have to watch over people and see they were doing everything right continuously. All I realised I had to do was write down each task step by step in the way I needed it performed, then let the person who was given the task follow my step by step guide, and just ask if they got stuck or needed help. That way I used this opportunity to make the instructions clearer for the next time.

The next stage was to show them how to perform a procedure and ask them to write the step by step guide, which was then turned into my systems and processes. Now I can give it to anyone to be able to do the job. I no longer have to worry about trusting anyone and whether they are doing it right. They just follow a working procedure. I agree this all sounds really simple, but you have to tweak it from the point of having 'good' systems and processes, to having 'better' systems and processes and, in time to the 'best' practice.

This procedure (better known as a system and process) can be followed by any person given a particular job, if it's been recorded. Even to the point of who's buying the milk would have a system and process, so there is always milk in the fridge should someone need it to make tea or coffee.

Now we have systems and processes in our business, the business can run itself and I do not need to be there all the time.

After building some S&P's I hired my first staff member to do some of the jobs I did and I was there to just back him up should there be any holes in the S&P's. Now I can get to work on exploring new avenues while my staff earn the money that I was once bringing in alone.

This led me to find out that a lot of my clients wanted to have support contracts. Before hiring a staff member this was another belief I had – that clients only wanted an instant fix when they called me, and were not prepared to wait their turn. Just as I'd believed they wanted onsite fixes and not remote support. The industry changed and so my business changed.

Working on my business I started rolling out the remote support plans to customers, setting a goal of just signing 5 per month. This snowballed to one month signing up 42 support plans! This was another big part of my business in making a residual income. These support plans led to more systems going in place and the business growing and needing to hire another staff member full time to do the accounts and renewals. The best part with all the systems and processes in place was that I still did not have to worry about trust as everyone was following the processes.

Of course, a change in my systems and processes, doing something different, was making a change that would give a different result. As I've learnt, it's all about "cause and effect".

The actions we took and changes we made, gave us some great results - over 60% increase in profits, and even better, more time off with family creating a better life balance. No longer was I working from 7am till 11pm, 7 days a week. I was taking days off to enjoy a hobby whilst my business continued to make me money.

A very wise man told me once, you don't run your business, systems and processes run your business and people run systems and processes.

***Chris Verbiest***

# 8 *SERVICE*

*Customer service is one of those things that everyone believes they are delivering in the best possible way! The truth is in most cases the opposite is very much the norm. I see so many businesses focus on getting the sale, doing the job, getting the money and then move onto the next customer with not a thought for the one that they have just serviced.*

*Customer service is so much more than that... For a start did you know that existing clients spend on average 33% more than new clients? That it costs, on average, six times more to get a new client than it does to get existing clients to buy your next product or service? Did you know that most businesses that fail to deliver a great customer service ultimately fail? If you don't look after your customers to an outstanding level then somebody else will!* **Ash**

I knew what I wanted to offer in my business and how I wanted to do it, but I didn't have a clear vision of how I would get there. I did not have long term goals; I ran my business day to day. Dealing with stuff as it came up and getting frustrated with constantly trying to move forward.

What I know now is I needed a vision. Having a clear vision is like knowing my destination right at the start. It is a powerful tool, which shows me where I want to be and helps me plan how I will get there. It's a bit like a sat nav, at the beginning of any journey, I put in where I want to go and bingo it takes me there.

I started the Millionaire Mindset in 2013 and was unsure as to why I really needed this, but something told me to listen to the guy telling me (constantly), "if you keep doing the same things then you'll continue to get the same results".

The guy in question was Ash Lawrence. I was fed up of going around in circles, and that's why I decided to be a part of this exciting business journey. I really wanted to move my business past the point of hard work, to a place where I could enjoy my business and also be in a position to help others too!

I was skint and to be completely honest I thought what the f**k am I doing! I'm struggling here and now I'm going to pay this guy money that I haven't really got! My husband was not impressed, ha ha. I remember trying to convince him, saying, "it'll be so much better, things will be different, trust me." This was something I often said about my business, so remembering the words Ash said, about doing the same thing getting the same result!

So I needed to do something different. I needed to run my business differently. I needed to have a different approach to get a different result, a positive result. I knew how to perform the service I offered but now it was the time to put that together with a business strategy. I'm excited to even be writing this, because knowing this really happened to me, means it could happen to you. Anyone that changes the way they run a business will get a result - a positive effect, or negative effect (depending on how they change it).

It was not easy and wasn't free from hurdles either; the hurdles were my unforgettable lessons. But it was an amazing journey that I'm still on today and the most important part is, I'm really enjoying the journey!

Being on the Millionaire Mindset not only gave me courage to continue with business, but also inspired me to grow and develop my knowledge and understanding of life. For example, the array of books we were advised to read. This was part of every month; a task to complete, and a book to read, and a buddy to chat with, keep on track with. The main objective was to take action and be accountable.

This was when I wrote my first vision and was clear about what I wanted my business and personal life to look like. So like the sat nav analogy I had direction.

What I learnt during my year on the Millionaire Mindset was vast. One part was about customer service which was right up my street. I love my business, I love what I do, I believe in the service I provide, so I wanted to be able to do it better, be the best, have people talking about my business, for clients to have a great experience.

I learnt that existing customers will spend 33% more than new customers. Information that was like gold dust to me, and I already had a fantastic client base which I felt so loyal too! I love my clients, I build a personal relationship with each client, and I'm on their journey with them. Ash explained one day, "someone you have done business with before, will spend with you again rather than a new customer". WOW I didn't realise how true this statement was. About 80% of my clients have unwanted hair, and as promised I clear the hair, leaving a permanent hair free area. I thought that would be it, the end of that client in my business but that's never the case.

Ash had made that statement, and yes indeed, clients want to stay with me, with my business. They are looking for the next thing that I can help them with. They ask me!!!! Because there is trust built between us. I'm truly grateful that I'm valued in this way, but it works both ways. I truly value my clients, because I genuinely care about each and every person.

I have learnt so much about customer service, knowing now that having a solid customer focus creates value for clients, this is so important. I want my clients to feel special; I want my clients to feel listened to. I've learnt that the client is boss! This statement makes me smile because when I first heard this I was a bit confused, how can my client be my boss?

So, what I now realise is; the client is always right, now that doesn't mean at the detriment of my business values or the service I provide. It means to ensure the client is provided with everything they need to have the best experience ever. If they are not clear about the service, time scale etc. then I haven't done my job properly. Being clear from the outset; having a caring friendly attitude, being approachable, listening to what my client really needs, in most cases it's such an emotional first meeting, giving a clear explanation of what I can do to help and how I do it.

Clarifying in detail questions that my client is unsure about. I was made aware of all these things, and just how important it is to any business. It costs 6 times more to get new clients than it does to keep the clients I already have. I've always done all the above as standard practice in my business, but didn't understand just how important it was. Happy clients equals repeat business and/or business referrals.

My business is about making a difference (I suppose this could be talking about any other business); OK I'll be more specific. I remove unwanted hair & skin lesions, a massive responsibility to perform and provide a great service; this is paramount to my business reputation and most importantly for the clients. The client trusts my every word and I know from my heart that I can achieve actually what I promise my clients.

Here you have it, a relationship starting to form at the very beginning, from the very first meeting. It's clear that the client feels confident that I can help them, and I'm clear that I will deliver. Now here's the thing- actually, just as I've explained my business analogy above, is how Ash Lawrence explained the business course to me. Well it was to a group of us really, but I felt he was talking directly to me! I believed him, I instantly trusted him. This is such an important part of a customer experience. Trust!

I finished my Millionaire Mindset course, with enthusiasm and excitement for the future but I just couldn't stop there. Learning is also about growth - with growth, change will happen. I need to change, I need to grow, I need continued support and encouragement to continue to grow!

I'm doing this with the **E**ntrepreneurs **B**usiness **C**lub.

Fellow business owners and the mind of Ash Lawrence help me to believe anything is possible. It's about commitment to my business, and commitment to the group. Doing what I say I'm going to do and showing up each month to be a part a real community of entrepreneurs.

My business today is a functioning profitable business. Am I really writing this? Wow yes I really am! I love my business and the clients in it. I now find I am constantly looking at ways to help improve and develop. I know that without accountability, checking in with people each month, I would be inclined to only do things that are easy, not risky and I wouldn't challenge myself. I have great ideas but sometimes fear, or feeling less than able, stops me in my tracks. This can cause me to procrastinate and avoid doing the main things that need to be done. Being accountable, having a clear goal and revisiting my "why" helps me to feel the fear and do it anyway!

The Entrepreneurs Business Club gives me this and more. If I stand still in fear then I fail to move forward for the beautiful new lessons for today. So I choose to move forward!

*Deborah Jones*

Should the amount of money spent influence the quality of the service you provide?

Service is that small seven letter word that has been the downfall of many businesses since business began. Whatever you sell, at whatever price you sell it for, you should always offer outstanding service. Get it wrong and you're screwed. Get it right and your business will flourish.

Simple, right?

The word service means many different things to each company but I'm going to deal with probably the toughest one out of all the services. The one that will absolutely make or break any business whether it's a start up one man band, or a century old multinational. I'm going to deal with the monster that is customer service.

Whatever product we supply whether it be a hotel room, car repair or selling toe nail clippers we all have customers. We may supply just a few customers or we may supply millions of customers but what every one of them expects is a certain level of customer service. The problem is every one of those customers will have different expectations, different wants, needs and tolerance of the service you provide.

I like to break down these customers into 3 tiers of service levels;

**Level 1**- Level one expect the best service but expect to pay for it.

**Level 1** customers are easy to deal with as their expectations match their financial ideas. You must provide a service that exceeds their expectations but you will have the budget and the resource to achieve it.

**Level 2-** Level two want a good service but expect to pay no more for it. They again are easy to deal with as they expect a good level of service but know what to expect for the money they spend. Again you should exceed expectations.

**Level 3** – Level three expect the best service but don't want to pay for it. They are the most dangerous to your business! They usually want to spend a relatively small amount of money but expect level 1 service. This can be a recipe for disaster and needs to be carefully managed, as even trying to exceed expectations may not fulfil their expectations.

This is just a simple break down of customers I have found over the years have given me the most issues. You could add many more levels but for now we will stick to the important three. Why? Because these are the most important, and identifying them could be critical to your business survival.

Now I know some of you will be saying great service should not be about how much they pay. I agree, everyone should have a great service and you should always exceed the expectations for the price point but as a business you have to set the expectations, and know your levels so you don't go bankrupt. For example if a level 1 customer came in looking for a wedding I know they would expect, and pay for, Champagne. Great no mismatch of expectations.

Level 2 would be quite happy with Prosecco as that's what they have paid for. Again great no mismatch of expectations.

Level 3 would expect Champagne for the price of lemonade! This is a problem as expectations are now mismatched. You could provide the Champagne but take a financial hit. Happy customers but your bottom line will take a hit.

Now this is an example using a certain product but it could also be related to the number of staff on the day to provide the service, surprise extras you give and the way the whole process is managed.

Again I'm not saying don't take the occasional financial hit to keep your customers happy but it's not a long term customer service strategy.

Many years of running a busy hotel has taught me much about how humans operate and how to read peoples expected levels of customer service. I can usually tell within 5 minutes of someone walking through the doors of my business if we are going to have a mismatch of expectations. I can usually allocate them a service level and manage them in slightly different ways.

Managing couples service levels who are looking for a wedding venue is always particularly challenging but a rewarding part of my daily job as a hotel manager. Couples would contact us with big ideas and dreams about their big day. They are excited and enthusiastic and so am I. If you're not as excited about a brides wedding as she is you should not be in the wedding industry.

From the first contact I have always endeavoured to give a service to the customer that exceeded the expectations they have of my business. We are a small family run establishment with a three star rating. I don't usually quote the star ratings as it's a little old fashioned now, but for this purpose it will give you an idea of what we are like and offer context - located in a slightly deprived part of Southern England. We hold about 60 weddings a year with a wide range of budgets between £500 -£10,000 each.

With such a wide range of budgets we deal with all three service levels on a regular basis, and we have mostly mastered managing the clients expectations.

Providing an outstanding service is the most important part of our business and this can be implemented irrespective of your customer level, or the depth of their wallets, but it is important to manage expectations from the start.

All our pre-wedding services are exactly the same whether you spend £500 or £10,000. This includes the first contact, unlimited advice and help with suppliers, general advice about how to make the day great, the quality of the literature, the coffee & cakes during our first meeting etc. etc. This is a low cost part of the service but helps everyone feel we are giving them an outstanding service. But what we are very careful to manage is the levels of expectations the couple have for the budget they want to spend.

The most important part of this exercise is honesty. Honesty with the customer and also honesty with yourself and your business. Don't offer or promise Champagne for lemonade money but do promise lemonade then add a surprising cherry on top that's unexpected!

Knowing our customer levels and managing expectations has helped reduce complaints and improve the service we offer. We know where each customer needs to be with their wants and needs but can also balance this against their budget.

Every customer receives a fantastic service that exceeds expectations but we don't bankrupt the business to achieve this. We simply add something on, that's over and above what they expect to receive.

***Roland Stanley***

By Entrepreneurs for Entrepreneurs!

Your reputation can be your most powerful marketing tool. A good reputation will sell your business for you, all you have to do is deliver. If you want a good reputation outstanding customer service is key.

*"You can't build a reputation on what you are going to do."*
- Henry Ford

Customer service could be described as the experience or journey that a customer or client has when interacting with your brand. We all strive to provide excellent services and products but it's occasionally important to take a step back and ask yourself, "do my clients or customers enjoy the experience?"

A business that understands good customer service would make sure that their client or customer is well looked after and happy throughout the entire process. Even if you provide the very best product or service possible, if your customer or client found the process difficult, annoying, or too time consuming, they're unlikely to come back.

One of the best pieces of advice to avoid this is to keep in contact with your clients and customers throughout their experience and let them know they can contact you. If your service is one that takes time, set regular "check in" times where you can update your customer or client on the work that's being done, and pre-warn them of anything that may cause a delay.

If your business has a quick customer experience like, for example an online shop, make sure there's a human available along the way. An online chat function can really help here. If you have employees, make sure you have solid systems and processes for them to follow so they don't just achieve the end result you want them to, but also do it the way you want them to. To keep your team motivated it's also important to reward for hard work and dedication to customer satisfaction.

If you look after you employees, they will look after your customers. Finally remember that the customer experience doesn't end after money has changed hands. Aftercare is just as important as the customer service that precedes it. It's sometimes a good idea to check back with a client or customer a few weeks after the sale to check that they are still happy. If they are it's a perfect time to ask for a testimonial.

A common challenge that modern businesses face is keeping up with the ever-changing demand and expectations of the customer, fueled by the internet. With vast amounts of information at peoples fingertips customers can easily research products and services that are right for them. However, because of this extensive amount of information, people's attention spans have become shorter.

As business owners it's our job to provide information as quickly as possible and make sure our customers find it easily. Again communication is the key here. On your website instant chat and video are excellent but even simple written FAQ's can make all the difference to a customer's experience. If you do business over the phone keep hold times to a minimum, and always return phone messages as soon possible.

Peoples reliance on the internet means that they expect you to have a strong online presence on your website, social media and other platforms. Make sure your company is being put across effectively and in conjunction with your brand values. Try not to spread yourself too thin. If you only have time to deal with, and communicate over one or two platforms, research the ones that are best suited to your business and concentrate on them.

We're often told as business owners to never say "no", but that's not the same thing as always saying "yes". We have to remember another common issue that businesses face is over promising and under delivering.

Knowing your industry and setting realistic timescales is very important in customer service. You don't have to say "no" but you can say "OK, but that would take us past the deadline", or "sure, but we'd need to revisit the price". It's best to have solutions ready for common requests or even practicing positive responses.

In the web design industry the two main pitfalls for designers are; deadlines being missed and promising the impossible, or at least the unachievable. We work hard towards ensuring project deadlines are met and even built a system that enables us and our client to keep track of a project's progress and communicate. On more than one occasion we've turned projects down either because the scope was too large or the deadline too tight. We think it's better to turn a project down than let a client down.

We regularly ask clients for feedback. This way we can either replace the areas of our customer service that aren't working and keep the things that are. It shows that you listen and have the willingness to change. After all we are constantly learning and your business is constantly changing. It's impossible to know everything but communicating effectively with your client means you can fix any problems before they arise.

With that in mind one hard truth that we must accept is that you can't always get everything right. No matter how hard you try, with all the best intentions, fact of the matter is, you will always come across a dissatisfied customer. Sometimes it's your fault, sometimes it's theirs, but in either case the best thing to do is manage the situation efficiently and politely.

It can be tough not to take things personally but try to hold your emotions in check. In some cases simply owning up to a mistake and fixing whatever issue has been created is enough to get things back on track. Sometimes you may find that the customer's personal life has caused them to lash out. In which case a polite and calm response can sometimes result in a positive outcome.

One example of a client experience that didn't go how we had planned was a few years back when our company was still developing. It wasn't anything that couldn't be easily resolved, but the client and I just didn't have the same ideas when it came to creating their company logo. I was aiming to attract prospective clients and had designed a logo to appeal to the clients target audience. The client wanted something that they liked the look of. The problem was that the client wasn't the target audience.

I started to lose a bit of confidence as everything I tried and explained just wasn't hitting the spot for them. I genuinely want each and every client to be left smiling. I could have just kept going and producing design after design but that would have just made us both more and more frustrated if it still wasn't 'correct'. We were communicating via email and I realised this was part of the problem. I called the client and we discussed options over the phone. We met up over coffee and realised it was simple miscommunication from the emails.

Once the client understood what we were aiming for they backed my designs and went on to launch a successful brand.

I learned a lot from the few client issues we faced in the beginning. The first lesson was to just listen. Don't interrupt, don't go on the defensive, (easily done when you built your business up over the years with your bare hands), but just listen and understand. A big part of making your clients experience with you a good one, is having that personal touch.

There's nothing worse for someone who's frustrated to be spoken over, or for the issue to just get passed from person to person without being resolved.

A great work ethic and a willingness to do what needs to be done, going above and beyond your call of duty is a key skill when providing the kind of service that people talk about. Some time ago one of our clients was holding a very important speech at an event that they were thrilled to be a part of. We had designed some promotional material for her attendees to take away with them after the speech.

Our client had organised her own printer who had assured her that the promotional material would be ready and waiting on location before she started speaking. We called our client just prior to the event to wish her good luck and she told us that the materials were not there. She sounded stressed as this was a vital part of her speech. We called the printers to see where our clients items were only to be told, they were still in the warehouse and wouldn't be delivered until later that evening on their next delivery run.

With a client deeply upset and just about to go on stage, we drove to the printers ourselves, collected the items and drove to the client's location just to catch the last 2 minutes of her speech with everything in hand, ready to distribute. This may seem like a small reason to be frantic, but it meant a lot to our client and she remains a repeat client even now.

Another piece of advice I would give is to give, yes give, without expecting to receive. Not only a business lesson but a life lesson as well. Giving a little can go a long way. Whether it's just offering advice, a free ebook/giveaway, fixing something for free, sharing valuable information that could help someone or even taking a long term client out for lunch every now and then.

Be good to loyal customers by giving them a shout out on social media, mention them and refer people to them. Give people your time and help, and you will be remembered!

*Carrie Stay*

# 9 *THE PEOPLE*

**Rachel Cowell...** (nee Rance) is joint business owner of JUSTSO Clothing & Merchandise Ltd, along with her husband Andrew. They have worked together for over 20 years and been married since 1992. Their business, JUSTSO, is all about getting businesses noticed and remembered in the best way with branding: branded workwear, uniform, sportswear and promotional items B2B and B2C. Branding is in her blood, as she started off her work career in marketing. So Rachel offers more than just branded products – she brings her expertise in brand development, and sales promotion too.

Rachel's passion for her business and enthusiasm for collaborative projects, encouraged her to take up her debut appearance in this book!

"Apart from anything else, it's always thrilling to have a new *first* at my age!" "They don't come around as often these days so you need to make the most of every opportunity!"

Hampshire born, in 1968, the youngest of 3 girls, Rachel lived in the UK until the age of 5,when she moved to Hong Kong. Her father was an airline pilot and his new job with Cathay Pacific Airways meant relocating there. She was very lucky to experience this lifestyle and feels blessed to have such great parents.

Aged 11 she was sent back to the UK for schooling and attended boarding school in Dorset. Commuting 1000's of miles by plane backwards and forwards every holiday gave her a thirst for travel, and she's still got plenty of destinations and experiences on her "bucket list". It also made her very independent and resourceful!

Next stop Kingston University where she studied for a BA Honours Degree in Business Studies for 4 years. With a 2.1 result, she landed a job straight away at a London sales promotion/marketing agency.

It was here she met her husband Andrew in 1991, and they've been combining a marriage with a business partnership ever since. A Mum to 2 fabulous children, (now adults) Lucy (23) and Harry (20), who she's so proud of. They inspire and drive her to be the best version of herself. "Dog Mum" to her furry baby, Alfie, the scruffy Border-Cairn Terrier cross who comes to work with her every day.

Loves all the usual stuff! Her ultimate vision is to live in her dream home right on the beach, building memories with family and friends!

By Entrepreneurs for Entrepreneurs!

**Carrie Stay...** along with Neil Dickson founded Clockwork Moggy in 2009 after completing their BA (hons) at UCA.

Whilst studying, I was working part time designing a music magazine. A fantastic job as I got to drive singers to gigs and met a few famous faces. The experience really helped to get a foot in the door in the design industry and led me to a full time job designing a lifestyle magazine. Although I enjoyed it, I really wanted variety and to have completely free reign on where design could take me. I wanted to make a real difference in helping other companies succeed. I've always quite liked the idea of running my own company, making my own way, so I took the leap, handed in my notice and Clockwork Moggy was launched.

We are a friendly team of myself, Carrie Stay (Branding/Graphic Designer), Neil Dickson (Web Designer Manager/Web Development) and Alicia Dickson (Online Marketing/SEO). We have an extensive knowledge of how branding and modern web design and graphic design can work for businesses with great results. We believe that through original and unique web and graphic design and online marketing, we will deliver a solution that suits you and your brand.

We do not use web templates or stock logos as we understand the importance of a company being able to stand out in a crowded market. It is our job to find a solution that represents your company effectively. We ensure that your branding gives prospective clients the right message, your website is ready for your visitors and your online marketing gives you great online presence on time, every time, LIKE CLOCKWORK.

In my spare time I enjoy a spot of kung-fu and occasionally like to practice axe throwing, archery and picking up some craft skills from the Viking era. If we ever have an apocalypse, I might just survive.

By Entrepreneurs for Entrepreneurs!

**Chris Verbiest...** Think Durex, Think Doctor, Think Yale…. I will cover your IT protection, remove any viruses if you've not been protected and bolt your doors to keep out the criminals. That's how I start my elevator pitch so you can remember me. Now I have implanted that in your head, you can ask me who I am?

I was born April 1971. Some say I may have had a lucky upbringing. My view is I had amazing parents that taught me right from wrong and supported me in anything I chose to do. It was never a rich family so to say I had everything I wanted was far from the truth. Everything I got or have now I work damn hard for. There's nothing like hard work to get want you want. So as for luck, I'd say I made my own.

After not doing the best at school I left with a few Grade 2's in CSE's, a 5 in English and Physics and funnily an Unclassified in computers. In 1987 I started a YTS at Queen Mary and Westfield College as a Jr Technician in the Computer Science and Physics department working towards a BTEC in Electronic Design. I struggled through 7 years and was finally told in the last year "we think you're dyslexic"! I still came out with a HND in Electronic Engineering. I continued to design electronics gadgets for the next 3 years then left to become a computer engineer for Computeq.

In 1998, in the middle of a recession, Verbo Computers was born. I worked on building a good customer base covering London Docklands and surrounding areas. Personally I met my wife in 2000, shortly followed by buying our first home, marrying and relocating to Kent in 2003, and it was at this time that our accountant advised us to become a Limited company. In 2005 I partnered with F-secure as a silver reseller (now a Gold partner). In 2006 our amazing daughter was born.

We plodded along happily for a number years- me earning a wage enjoying the freedom of running my own company. It was not until 2013, after the Millionaires Mindset course, that I had a hammer smash moment that woke me up. At this point I realised I was actually a business owner and did not want to continue being the only person working in my business. This is when my business life changed and it started to get really interesting and took on new direction.

*By Entrepreneurs for Entrepreneurs!*

**Deborah Jones...** is the managing director of Positive Pathways Beauty Ltd. She qualified as a beauty therapist over 20 years ago, as well as qualifying around the same time as an aerobic and fitness instructor. This was a major achievement for her because of her dyslexia. Retaining information was such a challenge and caused so many issues during school years. Leaving school with no qualifications she was over the moon, especially being a single parent at the time.

Deborah wanted to be the platform her children needed. Why? To give them drive and aspiration, motivation and hope, whilst developing her own self-worth and confidence. With this new self-belief, her ambitious nature and a keen desire to teach, she continued to study, achieving a degree, a Certificate in Education and she was elated, this fulfilled a childhood dream to teach beauty therapy.

Delighted, Deborah got offered a teaching position at Bexley College in Erith, Kent. She taught there for a number of years, also working as a mobile therapist running a small business. Her desire and passion for electrolysis was growing. Her vision was to have an electrolysis clinic. She knew to achieve this goal she would need to stop offering all other beauty services, and this would be a risky decision financially. Deborah, being an enthusiastic, positive and importantly a driven person, was prepared to take the risk knowing she would then be able to help so many people.

Today Deborah provides an electrolysis service at Positive Pathways to permanently remove unwanted hair. Changing many lives she is always humbled when clients give amazing feedback.

Deborah says, "Helping people to regain confidence, self-esteem and their self-worth is an amazing position to be in", she expresses with complete gratitude.

By Entrepreneurs for Entrepreneurs!

# Emily Hackett...

My passion in life is health and fitness and helping others achieve their goals. I believe that living a healthy lifestyle with regular exercise can change the way we feel about ourselves mentally and physically. Having trained as a professional dancer, fitness was a very important aspect of my career. However, I found myself living with an unhealthy diet and resenting exercise! My confidence was at rock bottom and this affected me in so many ways; bad skin, feeling fatigue, depression and seriously lacking motivation.

I then realised the only person that can make a real difference was ME! It was then my pain became my passion. I took a new career path in health and fitness where I studied to be a personal trainer. My love for fitness grew so much that I felt like it was time I pushed myself out of my comfort zone and did something that would completely change me as a person and leverage my reputation. In 2016 I won my PRO status as a professional fitness model for Pure Elite Body Building Federation. My goal now is to become a WBFF pro and compete internationally.

I have been in the industry for the last 2 years and in August 2016 I launched my own online coaching company called Body Transformation Academy, with my partner Ross Cowan. Our goal is to take 1:1 to 1 to many! We want to elevate ourselves in the industry and ultimately, help empower more people. Why help 10 people a day when you can help 10,000!

I believe if you're going to do something - do it to the best of your ability. Believe in focusing on the positives from every experience and enjoy inspiring others to achieve their goals.

# Entrepreneurs Business Club

By Entrepreneurs for Entrepreneurs!

**Roland Stanley...** is a multiple business owner, father, husband, serial VW camper owner and car tart born and raised in the Medway Towns, Kent just south of London.

From early on Roland always dreamed he would at some time own and run his own business and he achieved this by starting, writing and printing a local comic and magazine selling local bric-a-brac. Unfortunately at the age of 7, production of the magazine was halted due to lack of photocopying funds, and the general distractions such as playing with friends. The magazine's only sales stretched to 6 copies and the bric-a-brac section achieved the sale of one slightly rusty chest freezer. Profit £1.60 for the weekend.

However the family had a great tradition of starting multi-learning businesses so this was not going to be his last effort.

Both Roland's father and grandfather were business owners. George Stanley had been a serial entrepreneur since leaving school including building a large haulage company, hotel, structural engineering company, shipping wharfs and precision engineering company whilst his father Alan Stanley started several structural and architectural steel companies.

During the early 1990's the family took over the St George Hotel in Rochester. The hotel had been built in the 1960's but during most of the 1980's was leased out to another company.

Roland had just left school at this time and enrolled at catering college helping out at the hotel during the weekends. 3 years later he left the family business to work in France and several London and local restaurants as a chef but the opportunity to run his own business was still top priority.

Gaining vital experience Roland returned to the family business as head chef but the economic downturn had hit the hotel hard. Bankruptcy loomed but he dug in along with his father to turn it around. After 5 years Roland's father retired and left the business leaving Roland solely in charge with his good friend and general manager Clair Amos.

The hotel grew and became a successful business achieving great occupancy levels and holding many weddings. During this time Roland met his wife to be, Julie.

Roland now took charge of a small property portfolio the family had built up mainly by his grandfather. In 5 years he added 16 flats to the portfolio without borrowing any monies from outside the business.

In early 2017 the general management of the St George Hotel is in the hands of Clair, and Roland has turned his attention to a new project, co-working.

Dragon Co-working was born bringing together serviced offices and Co-working space and helping to connect people and encourage collaboration.

By Entrepreneurs for Entrepreneurs!

# Sally Marshall...

### October 2016

Trainer for Millionaire Mindset Course Training business owners on a 12 month course taking them from an employee to an entrepreneur mindset.

### 2014 – present

Author and business mentor. Working with small business owners helping them to free up their time and grow their businesses using the skills gained from working in the House of Commons. In 2015 published, **Delegate to Elevate**: 7 Steps to Success for Sole Traders followed by **Know Your Numbers:** How Is Your Business Performing? in May 2016.

Currently working on a book with Ash Lawrence, business psychologist, about networking.

### 2007 – 2010

Business Manager in the Department for Information Services, House of Commons, working on finance and performance management and reporting directly to the Board of Directors. Main achievement was to design a balanced scorecard which was implemented by the Directors to manage resources across the department. This was subsequently copied by other departments and I believe used across the whole House now.

### 1984 – 2007

Clerk's Department of the House of Commons working on various select committees and then moving up to become Departmental Finance Manager with an annual budget of £60m.

By Entrepreneurs for Entrepreneurs!

**Ross Cowan...** I really didn't start loving health and fitness. I hated the way I looked and dreaded social situations where I had to show my body. It was because of this I was never into sports and spent most of my youth being a little "toe rag" (my teachers words), getting into trouble, drinking, smoking and generally not looking after my body.

At the age of 21 I was a frail looking 8.5 stone. My only saving grace was being a naturally good swimmer.
I started working as a lifeguard at a leisure centre and decided to train myself plus a few friends too. After a few months we were getting some great results, members started asking me to train them over the other qualified PT's in the gym. I asked the manager if they could fund my PT qualification and they refused, so, I saved up the 3k for the course and did it myself.

Since then I've been lucky enough to change the lives of 100's of people, build an award winning PT studio from scratch, raise money for some awesome charities and have started taking home trophies from body building shows - first place and pro card coming in Nov 17 ;)

My passion now lies in teaching entrepreneurs the relationship between healthy eating and high performance. By surrounding myself with small teams of highly skilled, likeminded people I have rocketed my business forwards as well as collaborated to grow other peoples too. This is where its at, and we're going to keep building on it until we're working on an international level.

By Entrepreneurs for Entrepreneurs!

**Ash Lawrence...** Over the last thirty years, Ash has built up and sold four businesses. Ash owns Kent's fastest growing business network group, ABC Networks, as well as the Entrepreneurs Business Club. He is also a published author, STUFF for Business and Wily Old Fox Wisdom! He is also known as the #FlipFlopPsycho. (When you meet him you'll know why!)

He is a highly motivated individual, naturally enthusiastic with a real passion for life. He is totally dedicated and passionate about helping his clients achieve an extraordinary life. Ash believes that there are reasons and results, and reasons simply don't count!

Ash is a graduate of The Coaching Academy, also of the Masterclass of Corporate Coaching from The Coaching Academy. He is an NLP Practitioner, NLP Master Practitioner and NLP Master Trainer Trainer and was trained by some of the leading trainers in NLP including John Seymour, Paul McKenna, Michael Neil, and the creator of NLP Dr Richard Bandler. He is an EFT Master Practitioner and also has a PhD in Business and Sports Psychology. Philosophy is also at the heart of his learning. Ash is also a fully qualified Cognitive Behavioural Therapist (CBT).

Ash specialises in Mindset reprogramming for life success, business turnaround and cash generation.

Ash also achieved the ultimate goal for a sportsman, by playing for England 52 times and furthermore won a Silver Medal in the Indoor Cricket World Championships!! He also competed as a junior in the European Karate Championships.

He is an accomplished public speaker and holds monthly training courses in Business Growth, Psychology of Networking and Memory as well as his famous Millionaire Mindset SYSTEMS ©

Ash works with footballers in the Premiership and Football league. Also professional sports men and women in a variety of sports including cricket, swimming, athletics, golf and tennis. If you really want to be the best sportsman that you can be Ash will help you do it.

A lot of high net-worth individuals are really successful financially. However, some feel that they are not fulfilled and missing something important. Ash helps them "fill that gap!"

Most importantly, Ash is a genuine, honest and direct person. His life skills and experiences allow him to fully empathise with his clients on every level. Do not expect him to tell you what you want to hear.... Expect RESULTS!

# Resources

This where you can find loads of really useful books, articles and connections!
Please feel free to connect with any of the authors via their social media accounts.

Abcnetworks.co.uk
Ashlawrence.co.uk
Bta.fitness
Clockworkmoggy.com
Dragoncoworking.co.uk
Entrepreneurs Business Club
George-hotel.co.uk
Justso.biz
Millionaire Mindset course
Positive-pathways.co.uk
Reversethetide.com
STUFF for Business
Verbo.co.uk
Wily Old Fox Wisdom

The Go Giver by Bob Burg
The Go Giver Sells More by Bob Burg
How to Win Friends & Influence People by Dale Carnegie
The 10x Rule by Grant Cardone
The E-Myth Revisited by Michael Gerber
The Speed of Trust by Stephen Covey
The 3rd Alternative by Stephen Covey

www.ingramcontent.com/pod-product-compliance
Lightning Source LLC
Chambersburg PA
CBHW070237230526
45470CB00002B/443